Color in a
White Society

Color in a White Society

Barbara W. White, Editor

Selected Papers
from the NASW Conference
Color in a White Society
Los Angeles, California, June 1982

National Association of Social Workers, Inc.
Silver Spring, Maryland

Cover design by Johanna Vogelsang
Interior design by Susan B. Laufer

Copyright © 1984, National Association of Social Workers, Inc.
First Impression, 1989

Library of Congress Cataloging-in-Publication Data

NASW Conference: Color in a White Society (1982 :
    Los Angeles, Calif.)
    Color in a white society.

    Includes bibliographies.
    1. Social work with minorities—United States—
Congresses.   2. Social work education—United States—
Congresses.   I. White, Barbara W.   II. National
Association of Social Workers.   III. Title.
HV3199.U62N37   1984   362.8′4′0973   84-19051
ISBN 0-87101-128-X

Printed in the United States of America

Preface

It is appropriate that *Color in a White Society* should be the first book published by the National Association of Social Workers (NASW) following my appointment as the association's executive director, for this volume deals with issues and concerns that have been of long-standing interest to me on a personal as well as a professional level.

The articles presented here confirm that people of color still face problems in the United States—problems that are manifold and diverse, ranging from the ambiguous status of Mexican aliens to the high rate of infant mortality in the black community. Also significant and challenging are the color-related problems that apply to social workers in their own practice and in their own national organization. Conspicuous among our needs as NASW members is the development and adoption of an ethnic-sensitive focus for our practice.

The issue of paramount importance for NASW is answering the needs of its membership, many of whom are minorities. In my view, the association can better serve its minorities in the following ways:

1. We must represent the profession's minorities, acknowledging their diversity and contributions.

2. We must become a repository of hard data and usable information on members of color and their historical relationship to social work practice. The present volume is a beginning example of how NASW's program departments and its publications department can work together to reach this goal.

3. We must extend the role of the association in professional regulation as related to minorities. The aim would be to reach out creatively and bring into the professional family all specialized groupings of minority social workers.

4. We must conduct a program of public reeducation to create a clearer, more favorable image of minorities in the profession. The objectives should include dispelling myths and creating and institutionalizing new, accurate images.

It is hoped that if we explore and utilize the preceding approaches to put our own house in order, we will learn lessons and develop techniques that we can apply to the broader problems of white society itself.

In any case, the present volume is a demonstration that there is within NASW a breadth of vision, a depth of scholarship, and a general articulateness that can define and help alleviate the frequently difficult conditions faced by this nation's people of color.

I commend the efforts of Editor Barbara White, the contributing authors, and others in NASW who helped produce this volume. Further, I invite readers to work with me toward meeting the goal of developing color and ethnic competence among those who work in the nation's social welfare system.

Mark G. Battle
Executive Director, NASW

August 1984

Contents

Introduction

*If freedom and equality are not vouchsafed
the peoples of color, the war for democracy
will not be won.*
A. Philip Randolph, "Why Should We March?"

When A. Philip Randolph, the respected and revered civil rights leader, wrote these words it was in reference to another era in the quest for realizing the ideal of equality in the social, political, and economic affairs of this country. Conventional wisdom and, more recently, neoconservative ideology state that sufficient progress has been made in improving the iniquitous situation of people of color in the United States. The implementation of affirmative action policies, for example, has led a large number of Americans to believe that more than enough has been accomplished. Yet, the striking antithesis of such perceptions is that many Americans continue to exist in a social chasm, the formal causes of which are no great secret to anyone—hunger, housing, crime, illness, and lingering patterns of political and economic oppression. Without exception, this chasm is disproportionately inhabited by people of color.

Racism, in its personal, professional, and institutional forms, permeates the life situations of ethnic minorities—as citizens seeking to preserve their rights and as clients of social service agencies. Changes in social policy have reflected a reversal of this country's commitment to justice and equity for oppressed people. This changed mood is being expressed more vividly in the 1980s.

The problems of people of color are long lived, profound, and often complex. Solutions will not be simple. However, without an immediate recognition of the impact of these problems, it is doubtful that any lasting solutions will be forthcoming.

Social work is no stranger to these issues. It has traditionally been looked to for leadership and support in altering conditions that impede human potential and dignity. Some believe that the efficacy of traditional social work approaches is, at best, questionable in meeting the needs of ethnic minority populations. Such opinions have seemed to fluctuate with changes in the emphases of social work practice through the years.

The goals of the profession have always expressed basic humanitarian principles, societal change, and the alleviation of distress and suffering. But ethnic minority social workers are saying to the profession as a whole that it must increase its recognition of the need to conceptualize, understand, and use ethnicity as an essential component of its knowledge base if social work is to live up to its noble purpose. From this perspective the profession must not neglect to take advantage of the knowledge and experiences of minority researchers, educators, and practitioners as conduits of the operational realities of its values and methods. To do so would be to disregard a potential for productivity, creativity, and problem solving in the search for strategies to ameliorate injustice in society.

The National Association of Social Workers (NASW) has sought to incorporate the concerns of ethnic minority social workers and clients into its various programs and has acknowledged and confirmed its commitment to respecting diversity in a pluralistic society. NASW tries to recognize its responsibility to help eradicate racism and discrimination wherever they occur in society, including NASW's interorganizational affairs. Yet, despite the rhetorical attention given these issues, a significant number of minority social workers, both members and nonmembers, have believed that NASW was inimical to the concerns of minority members and minority clients.

NASW's sponsorship of "Color in a White Society" changed some of these views. The conference was perceived by many participants to be a significant event for NASW. The success of the conference may help foster a broader recognition of NASW's potential as an advocate for the concerns of people of color.

NASW's National Committee on Minority Affairs (NCOMA) conceptualized a conference that would address the concerns of people of color and direct national attention to the issues which persist because of racism and its institutional manifestations. Through NCOMA's work in past years, it had become evident that a major forum was needed to provide exposure for the work of ethnic minority social workers. With the approval and support of the NASW national Board of Directors, "Color in a White Society"—the First National Conference on Minority Issues in Social Work—was convened in Los Angeles, California, June 9–12, 1982.

The enthusiastic response to the call for papers allowed the Conference Planning Committee the luxury of being able to select a wide array of topics that exemplified high-quality work. The subjects gave attention to the various fields of social work practice and comprehensive social issues. Eighty-six workshops, panels, and papers were presented, including preconference institutes and invitational presentations that were attended by over 750 individuals. The majority of those in attendance were members of the largest ethnic minority groups in NASW: Asian Americans, American Indians, black Americans, Chicanos, and Puerto Ricans. The ethnic composition of NCOMA and of the Conference Planning Committee was a microcosm of these groups.

Since its inception, the work of NCOMA made clear the mutuality of the concerns of ethnic minority groups, all of whom are victimized by discrimination. The uniqueness of the conference as a fusion of diverse groups raised interesting questions for the planners. We asked ourselves: What are the identifiable issues that crosscut each group's perspective of its unique concerns? How can we best convey the experiences and successful efforts of particular groups to others with similar problems? Can we begin to build a bridge that will lead to greater understanding and appreciation of and among people of color? How can we begin to actuate networks and coalitions in relation to practice and policy initiatives?

The idea of coalitions and networking has been assumed feasible and desirable for movement toward shared goals of a common humanity. This conference was an important step toward testing the grounds on which ethnic minority coalitions can be viable.

Part of what emerged was the recognition that there is no one political philosophy that characterizes the commonality of ethnic minority groups. There is no one way of looking at the world that is officially prescribed and to which all groups must adhere. Yet, the intensity of the cause can provide a sense of community and alliance for them while permitting them to retain their diversity.

It was apparent that the conference went beyond the traditional didactic approaches to events of this nature. The opportunity that was made available for exchange and learning was equalled by the goal of giving encouragement and appreciation to social workers of color who may be faced with frustration or ennui as they carry out their roles as service providers and advocates for equity in a frequently hostile environment. As attested to by those in attendance, this goal was fulfilled. Throughout the conference, there prevailed an atmosphere of purpose along with personal and intellectual stimulation.

Several major themes appeared in the multifarious agenda. Many of the distinguished speakers reemphasized that the national pathology of racism and sexism are amazingly resilient. This fact calls for the continuous exposure of inequities wherever they exist as barriers to human functioning. Another theme was the reminder that professionals must not overlook the inherent strengths of the various groups of people of color. Indigenous community institutions, cultural patterns, and heritages, and the innate strengths of people of color are valuable resources for social workers. It was strongly stressed that social workers need to recommit themselves to the continuous quest for the survival of clients, peers, and agencies during this period of diminishing resources. The special situations of the refugee-immigrant populations and affirmative action were correctly predicted to be salient issues in the 1980s. Another prominent theme was the discussion and reaffirmation of the need to continue to refine and promote the integration of knowledge and skills specific to the needs of the ethnic minority clients and workers that are essential to the advancement of social work practice. The working agenda was to find ways to assure that the vital but no less crucial concerns of the exploited, the alienated, and the powerless are not excluded from the nation's priorities.

The articles chosen for this volume reflect the diversity of the issues raised at the conference. They illustrate the range and substance of this special event. It is my hope that these articles will inspire others who are continuing to validate and sustain these serious issues that effect all Americans. The inscription "Novus Ordo Seclorum"—a new order of the ages—is written on the Great Seal of the United States. Let us not miss the opportunity to assure that a "new order" becomes a reality for people of color.

BARBARA W. WHITE

August 1984

Acknowledgments

Many individuals invested so much of themselves in making this "first" conference a reality. The service of all past members of the National Committee on Minority Affairs (NCOMA) provided the conscience and inspiration for this effort. I extend to them my appreciation for their experience and wisdom. Special words of gratitude for her leadership are extended to Adel Martinez, who served as chairperson of NCOMA when the conference was being planned. The members of NCOMA from 1980 to 1982 provided the team spirit, hard work, and dedication that were necessary to attain our objectives. I also want to acknowledge the work of the individuals who donated their time to review the abstracts submitted for the conference and those who reviewed the articles submitted for this volume.

My thanks are due and are gratefully expressed to the following NASW staff members whose capable efforts produced an outcome of which we can all be justifiably proud: Jim Evans, Sheldon Goldstein, Georgianna Carrington, Charisse Young, Sharon Chelnick, and Shirley Ford. I also thank the members of the Conference Planning Committee, who gave unstintingly of their time and knowledge, and the editorial staff of NASW, who were involved in the production of this volume.

Contributors

Positions are those held at the time of the conference (June 1982)

Rodolfo Arroyo, MSW, Social Worker, Social Work Department, Ben Taub General Hospital, Houston, Texas.

Emily Bruce, Research Assistant, Northwest Regional Child Welfare Training Center, School of Social Work, University of Washington, Seattle.

Leon W. Chestang, Ph.D., Dean, School of Social Work, Wayne State University, Detroit, Michigan.

Pamela Day, MSW, Project Coordinator, Northwest Regional Child Welfare Training Center, School of Social Work, University of Washington, Seattle.

Ismael Dieppa, DSW, Dean, School of Social Work, Arizona State University, Tempe.

Arthur Dodson, MSW, Director, Casey Family Program, Western Washington Division, Seattle.

Joseph S. Gallegos, Ph.D., Assistant Professor and Project Coordinator, Multi-Ethnic Mental Health Training Project, School of Social Work, University of Washington, Seattle.

Lawrence E. Gary, Ph.D., Director, Institute for Urban Affairs and Research, Howard University, Washington, D.C.

Jewelle Taylor Gibbs, Ph.D., Assistant Professor, School of Social Work, University of California, Berkeley.

Bogart R. Leashore, Ph.D., Research Associate, Institute for Urban Affairs and Research, Howard University, Washington, D.C.

Dorothy M. Linder, MSW, Executive Director, Delaware State Chapter, National Association of Social Workers, Wilmington.

Sandra A. López, MSW, Social Worker, Social Work Department, St. Joseph Hospital, Houston, Texas.

Carol Hill Lowe, MSW, Associate Chief of Maternal and Child Health, Commission of Social Services, District of Columbia Department of Human Services, Washington, D.C.

Chizuko Norton, MSW, Lecturer, School of Social Work, University of Washington, Seattle.

Martha N. Ozawa, Ph.D., Professor, George Warren Brown School of Social Work, Washington University, St. Louis, Missouri.

Ramón M. Salcido, DSW, Associate Professor, School of Social Work, University of Southern California, Los Angeles.

Linda Wilson, MSW, Social Worker and Project Coordinator, Cross-Cultural Training, Casey Family Program, Western Washington Division, Seattle.

National Committee on Minority Affairs, 1981–82

Leon W. Chestang, Chair
Detroit, Michigan

E. Diane Johnson
Wellesley, Massachusetts

Creigs Beverly
Atlanta, Georgia

Patricia L. Salcido King
Chevy Chase, Maryland

Dorothy Chu
New York, New York

Madeline Krimmel
Springfield, Virginia

Martha Fimbres
Tucson, Arizona

Judith Morales
Montclair, New York

Tsuguo Ikeda
Seattle, Washington

Ramón M. Salcido
Los Angeles, California

Conference Planning Committee, 1981–82

Barbara White, Chair
Tallahassee, Florida

Martha Fimbres
Tucson, Arizona

E. Diane Johnson
Wellesley, Massachusetts

Roberto Ruiz
Teaneck, New Jersey

Angela Shen-Ryan
New York, New York

The Ethnic Competence Model for Social Work Education

Joseph S. Gallegos

Social work practitioners who lack the skills, attitudes, and knowledge to work effectively in cross-cultural settings are incompetent. And schools that continue to graduate social workers who are unprepared for such practice are irresponsible. This charge is not new. It has been the primary concern of minority social workers at least since the 1960s. What is new is that over the past twenty years, through the arduous work of numerous minority scholars, there has been a breakthrough in defining those competencies for practice. Thus, minority scholars are rapidly moving toward expanatory models that will allow minority educators and practitioners to share what they know and to transmit this knowledge to those who plan curricula.

BACKGROUND

Before discussing the ethnic competence model, it will be useful to review briefly the role of the Council on Social Work Education (CSWE) and its Commission on Minority Groups in these developments. In 1968, CSWE adopted what would become the controversial minority accreditation standard, which required all schools to establish cultural diversity in the enrollment of students, the hiring of faculties, and the establishment of curricula. A minority task force was established, which later evolved into the Commission on Minority Groups. The commission is composed of social work educators who represent each of the major ethnic minority groups of color—American Indians, Asian Americans, blacks, and Hispanics.

The commission, through its sponsorship of numerous task forces, workshops, training programs, reports, and publications, has continued to make significant contributions to minority social work education in spite of the erosion of interest in and the resources given to this issue over the past few years. The commission's original charge was to inform and advise CSWE on matters pertaining to minority interests in relation to faculty, students, and curricula. That charge was recently reaffirmed by CSWE, as was the commitment to the struggle against racism and to social justice for minorities.

The recently proposed new accreditation standards and policy on curricula are evidence that CSWE and the commission will continue to champion that cause. A careful study of these two regulatory documents indicates that the concern for measurement and the identification of specific social work competencies is not limited to minority educators. In that vein, the emerging works of minority writers have a value which transcends their own interest groups. More directly, as minority scholars continue to define cross-cultural competence in social work toward the goal of equal services for *all* Americans, all will benefit.

Although the issue of competent practice with minorities has been an underlying issue, it has taken social work a long time to get beyond a statement of the problem. In the early years, minorities had to struggle merely to have information on their history and identity incorporated into the social work curricula. However, when such information was included, it was done in a disjointed manner, without explanation, and thus lacked consistency. Nonminority instructors, who had little knowledge in this area, often borrowed bibliographies from the history, political science, or other departments and attached them to their social work bibliographies. Hence, there was little real change in the curricula as it had existed up to that time.

During the mid-1970s, minority scholars took up the challenge, and a growing literature on theoretical frameworks began to emerge. They did so in direct response to the charge by nonminority scholars that the content on minorities lacked a theoretical base and, therefore, lacked parity with other substantive content areas. The next barrier to the infusion of minority content was the charge that it was not an organized curriculum. In the past five years, organized curricula in almost every area of minority social work have been developed—in aging, child welfare, substance abuse, and so on.[1] The latest barrier seems to be couched in a "so-what" attitude.

So what if one is armed with theory and knowledge, how does one translate that information into effective practice? This is the very question that minority scholars are now pursuing.

ETHNIC COMPETENCE

Underlying Assumptions

Before addressing directly the concept of ethnic competence, some underlying assumptions are in order. The focus of this work is on ethnic minorities of color. To think in global terms about such diverse groups, one must first establish a unifying framework that respects the uniqueness of each minority group and recognizes the diversity within each group. In attempting to develop such a framework, the author was concerned less with the issues pertaining to specific groups, than with universal concepts that seem to cut across ethnic lines and address common issues. A framework for discussing universal concepts is as follows:

1. Minorities of color share a history of discrimination and oppression based primarily on color and cultural differences from the mainstream population.

2. Unlike the mainstream culture, which is predominantly Western, the ancestral roots of these groups are non-Western.

3. The life experiences of these groups are typified by socio-cultural dissonance.

Beyond the notion of what is universal is the concept of pluralism. That is, the United States is a pluralistic society composed of many social and cultural groups who have divergent interests. Although the structure of this society is pluralistic, the process of socialization does not respect cultural differences. As a result, those who are culturally "different" experience sociocultural dissonance. If one accepts these assumptions about universal concepts and pluralism, one can begin to develop an accommodating explanatory model that can serve as a foundation from which to build a training curriculum that addresses the needs of minorities.

"Ethnic competence" is the mastery of relevant knowledge and skills, including insights and experiences, that can be used in any cross-cultural situation, regardless of the client's or worker's ethnic group.[2] Thus, an "ethnically competent" worker is able to function effectively in more than one culture. It is acknowledged that, for the average person, simply adjusting and adapting to one culture is often a life-long process. Nevertheless, for the helping professional in a pluralistic society, ethnic competence must be an educational goal.

Ethnic Competence Procedures

Ethnic competence is not simply empathy for minority persons; nor is it limited to specific interpersonal skills. Rather, it is a set of procedures and activities to be used in acquiring culturally relevant insights into the problems of minority clients and the means of applying such insights to the development of intervention strategies that are culturally appropriate for these clients. Green et al. have identified the following procedures:

- Clarification of the worker's personal values concerning minority persons.
- Articulation of personal and professional values and ways they may conflict with or accommodate the needs of minority clients.
- The development of interviewing skills that reflect the worker's understanding of the role of language in ethnically distinct communities.
- The development of the ability to relate to minority professionals in ways that enhance their effectiveness with clients.
- The development of the ability to use resources—agencies, persons, research—on behalf of minority communities.
- The development of the mastery of techniques for learning the history, traditions, and values of a minority group.
- The development of the ability to communicate information on the cultural characteristics of a given group to other professionals.
- Gaining knowledge of the impact of social policies and services on minority clients.[3]

Ethnic competence requires sensitivity and awareness in the assessment of the cultural implications and influences of the help-seeking process. Much of what distinguishes one culture from another—and differentiates subcultures in a large pluralistic sociey such as this—are the diverse ways that people perceive and report their experiences, including stress and crises. Communication is an obvious cultural factor, as is the fact that people experience a problem or crisis as both a personal and a social event. Therefore, a culturally sensitive intervention model must account for the role of language, socialization, and socially significant others in the diagnosis and evaluation of personal problems. Consideration of two concepts will help illustrate these points—the dual perspective and a help-seeking-behavior model.

Dual Perspective

The dual perspective is the conscious and systematic process of perceiving, understanding, and comparing simultaneously the values, attitudes, and behavior of the larger societal system with those of the client's immediate family and community system. It requires substantive knowledge of and empathy toward both systems, as well as an awareness by the social worker of his or her attitudes and values. Thus, the dual perspective allows one to experience each system from the point of view of the other.[4]

The concept of the dual perspective stems from the idea that all persons are part of two systems: the larger societal system and their immediate environment. The task of the ethnically sensitive social worker is to assess the degree of congruence or incongruence between the two systems. The achievement of congruence for ethnic minorities, in a society that devalues their immediate environmental system, is difficult. Yet, when congruence is found, it is likely that the strengths of the systems can be identified. Whether the systems are congruent or not, useful cues for intervention can be discerned, and it is this aspect that makes the dual perspective uniquely suited for working with ethnic minorities.

Help-Seeking-Behavior Model

Another concept that demonstrates the importance of and potential pitfalls in cultural assessment is the help-seeking-behavior model reported by Green et al.[5] As the dual perspective depicts the structure of the minority client or client system in situation, the help-seeking model illustrates the helping process.

Five major components of this model are relevant for cross-cultural encounters. The first component is that the client's definition of problems will likely vary from that of the social worker who comes from another culture. Different world views and social experiences color how each one interprets and articulates experiences. The worker has a particular cultural set that often is at variance with the client's—especially a client whose culture is different. The second component is that a successful intervention uses labels, words, or concepts that are familiar and acceptable to the client in defining the problem; it involves more than a common language and refers more broadly to cultural understanding. It implies, for instance, that a client may receive greater satisfaction from a folk healer than from an insensitive clinician. The third component is

similar to the second, but applies the same idea to indigenous intervention strategies, which the ethnically competent worker utilizes
when feasible. The fourth component is that the worker knows
how to obtain and use the necessary cultural information and
resources. Once the ethnically competent worker gains this
knowledge, he or she will use it and share it with clients and colleagues. The fifth component stresses the expectations and values
of the community in the assessment of outcomes of intervention.
Treatment can only be considered successful if it is evaluated as
such by the clients and their community.

The thrust of the help-seeking-behavior model and the dual perspective is that social workers must work hard to understand the
complexities presented by cultural differences. They must free
themselves from their own cultural bonds to make the helping interaction congruent with the client's framework of understanding and
acceptance.

Empowerment

The third major aspect of the ethnic competence model is empowerment. The ethnically competent worker must be concerned with
the goal of social work with all minorities, which is empowerment.
Solomon described empowerment, whether directed toward a client,
a community, or a colleague, as the process by which persons who
belong to a stigmatized social category throughout their lives can
be assisted to develop and increase their skills in the exercise of
interpersonal influence and the performance of valued social roles.[6]

Empowerment is used in this model as a generic base or a value
that can be both a process and a goal. As a process, it refers to
the interaction between a social worker and client or client system
in which both parties are empowered. Ideally, the client system
is empowered by a sensitive and ethnically competent social worker,
and the social worker is empowered by this interaction in that his
or her skills and resources in reaching across cultural barriers are
enhanced by each experience. Empowerment also may extend to
interaction among colleagues; in this sense, it refers to the respect-
ful relationship between minority and nonminority professionals,
such as intellectual exchanges between minority and nonminority
practitioners or the exchange of resources between agencies and
minority communities. The style and manner of these exchanges
can, in themselves, be empowering.

The goal of empowerment, as it is more commonly understood,

is to increase the exercise of interpersonal influence and effective social functioning. Thus, empowerment can be used to facilitate a client system's self-perception as a causal force capable of influence and direction. However, it must be recognized that empowerment does not mean to give someone power. Rather, it is an act of facilitating a client's (or client system's) connection with his or her own power. Cultural sensitivity, knowledge, and ethnic competence will provide the worker with cues to determine the client system's power base and structure.

SKILLS OF ETHNIC COMPETENCE

This section lists the attributes, knowledge, and skills that are necessary for ethnically competent practice.[7]

Personal Attributes

■ Personal qualities that reflect genuineness, empathy, non-possessive warmth, and the capacity to respond flexibly to a range of possible solutions.
■ An acceptance of and openess to differences among people.
■ A willingness to learn to work with clients of different ethnic minority groups.
■ Social workers' articulation and clarification of their personal values, stereotypes, and biases about their ethnicity and social class, as well as those of others, and ways they may accommodate or conflict with the needs of ethnic minority clients.
■ Personal commitment to alleviate racism and poverty.

Knowledge

The ethnically competent social worker gains knowledge in the following areas:
■ The culture (history, traditions, values, family systems, and artistic expressions) of ethnic minority clients.
■ The impact of clients and ethnicity on behavior, attitudes, and values.
■ The help-seeking behaviors of ethnic minority clients.
■ The role of language, speech patterns, and communication styles in various ethnic communities.
■ The impact of social service policies on ethnic minority clients.
■ The resources (agencies, persons, informal helping networks,

and research) that can be utilized on behalf of ethnic minority clients and communities.

■ The ways that professional values may conflict with or accommodate the needs of ethnic minority clients.

■ Power relationships in the community, agencies, or institutions and their impact on ethnic minority clients.

Skills

The skills required for ethnically competent practice include the ability to do the following:

■ Establish techniques for learning the cultures of ethnic minorities.

■ Communicate accurate information on behalf of ethnic minority clients and their communities.

■ Discuss openly racial and ethnic differences and issues and respond to culturally based cues.

■ Assess the meaning of ethnicity for individual clients.

■ Differentiate between the symptoms of intrapsychic stress and stress arising from the social structure.

■ Master interviewing techniques that reflect an understanding of the role of language in the client's culture.

■ Utilize the concepts of empowerment on behalf of ethnic minority clients and communities.

■ Use resources on behalf of ethnic minority clients and their communities.

■ Recognize and combat racism in and racial stereotypes and myths held by individuals and institutions.

■ Evaluate the validity and applicability of new techniques, research, and knowledge for work with ethnic minorities.

The foregoing list marks the current stage in the ability to define ethnic competence. Similar contributions have been made by Cleckley and by Munoz.[8] The next step is to define the knowledge, skills, and attitudes on this list in behavioral terms. The challange is great, but the achievement of such a task can be the most significant breakthrough in the movement toward social work education for practice with minorities. Such a taxonomy of ethnic competence will permit the development of tools for accountability by schools, agencies, and practitioners.

Just as competence in the delivery of services to minorities always has been an issue for minorities in social work, the main barrier to the equitable receipt of services has been institutional racism. Armed with the tools of accountability, social workers who are sympathetic to minority issues will be better equipped to advocate on behalf of their needs. Before this can occur, however, research that validates the numerous theories about work with minorities must take place. The minority commission of CSWE continues to contribute to this effort through its successful program for training doctoral-level minority researchers and mental health administrators whose goal must be empowerment. The aim of empowerment is not only to enable nonminorities to work more effectively and competently with minorities, but to help minorities to bridge the gap in cross-cultural understanding and to determine their own agendas in social work education and practice.

Notes and References

1. See, for example, *Providing Child Welfare Services in a Multi-cultural Society* (Washington, D.C.: Creative Associates, 1981); Frank F. Montalvo et al., *Mexican American Culture Simulator for Child Welfare: Case Vignettes* (San Antonio, Tex.: Our Lady of the Lake University of San Antonio, 1981); and *A Manual to Facilitate the Infusion of Ethnic Minority Aging Content into the Base of Social Work Education Curriculum* (New York: Council on Social Work Education, March 1980).

2. For examples of ethnic competence as an emerging concept, see Wynetta Devore and Elfriede Schlesinger, *Ethnic-Sensitive Social Work Practice* (St. Louis: C.V. Mosby Co., 1981); James W. Leigh, Jr., "Directions for the Future: The Ethnic Competent Social Worker," in Ellen S. Saalberg, ed., *A Dialogue on the Challenge for Education and Training: Child Welfare Issues in the '80's* (Ann Arbor: National Child Welfare Training Center, University of Michigan School of Social Work, 1982), pp. 43–55; Susan Medina et al., *Fresno Hispanic Permanency Planning Demonstration Project* (Los Angeles, 1982); and Jacquelyn Dupont Walker, *Ethnic Minority Cultures—Shades of Difference* (Ann Arbor: National Child Welfare Training Center, University of Michigan School of Social Work, 1982).

3. James W. Green et al., *Cultural Awareness in the Human Services* (Englewood Cliffs, N.J.: Prentice-Hall, 1982), pp. 53–66.

4. Dolores G. Norton, *The Dual Perspective* (New York: Council on Social Work Education, 1978), p. 3.

5. Green et al., *Cultural Awareness in the Human Services*, pp. 28–48.

6. Barbara Solomon, *Black Empowerment* (New York: Columbia University Press, 1976).

7. Linda Wilson, "Ethnic Competence: Skills, Attitudes, Knowledge." Unpublished paper, Multi-Ethnic Mental Health Training Project, School of Social Work, University of Washington, Seattle, 1982.

8. Faye U. Munoz, *Manpower Considerations in Providing Mental Health Services to Ethnic Minority Groups* (Boulder, Colo.: Western Interstate Commission on Higher Education, 1980); and Betty J. Cleckly, "Education for Practice with Blacks," *Journal of Humanics*, 8 (1980), pp. 17–33.

Trends in Social Work Education for Minorities

Ismael Dieppa

The trends in social work education for minorities can be meaningful only if they are examined within a framework that includes five perspectives. The first perspective is the progress made in the last twenty years in implementing accreditation standard 1234A adopted by the Council on Social Work Education (CSWE) in 1971. This standard requires schools of social work to make special efforts to enrich programs by providing racial, ethnic, and cultural diversity in the composition of the student body, faculty, and curriculum design. The second perspective is the systematic development and utilization of a body of knowledge about ethnic minority perspectives in the social work curriculum. The third perspective is the demonstrated knowledge and competence of faculties in schools of social work in relation to the ethnic minority experience; the sociocultural attributes of blacks, Chicanos, Asian Americans, American Indians, and Puerto Ricans; and the struggle of these groups for self-determination and empowerment in a frequently hostile environment. The fourth perspective is the development of social services controlled by ethnic minority communities that could provide a viable field placement for students. The fifth perspective is the sociopolitical stance of the social work profession, as manifested in an increasingly conservative society.

GENERAL TRENDS

Social work education has experienced a phenomenal growth in the last three decades.[1] From 1952 to 1962, schools of social work

10

awarded MSW degrees to 18,604 students and doctoral degrees to 189 students. From 1962 to 1972, the growth of the profession was more significant. During that time, 45,003 students received MSWs and 705 students received doctoral degrees. However, the most significant growth in the number of graduate degrees awarded took place from 1972 to 1981. During that period, 81,706 students received an MSW degree and 1,575 received doctorates.

In addition, undergraduate social work education emerged and mushroomed during the thirty-year period (1952–82). In 1956, there were 90 undergraduate programs affiliated with CSWE. By 1975, 142 accredited undergraduate programs had awarded 6,704 degrees. The significant growth continued through 1981, when 301 accredited programs awarded 8,343 BSW degrees. To illustrate the rapid development of baccalaureate education, it suffices to observe that the enrollment of full-time BSW students increased from 22,966 in 1975 to 29,350 in 1978.

It should be noted that CSWE began to publish statistics on the ethnic characteristics of social work students in 1970. Judging by the small number of ethnic minority social workers practicing in the 1960s, one is led to conclude that few ethnic minority students were entering and graduating from schools of social work during that time. However, the efforts of a few ethnic minority social workers and the timely response by CSWE and schools of social work during the civil rights decade (1962–72) gave impetus to a trend of increased recruitment of ethnic minority students at the BSW, MSW, and doctoral levels. James R. Dumpson, then president of the CSWE Board of Directors, set forth the need for a commitment to address issues and problems related to ethnic minorities in his message to the CSWE House of Delegates. He stated the following:

> It is my view, shared I know, by the CSWE Board, staff and members of the Special Committee on Minority Groups, that there is no matter of greater concern and importance than the recruitment into social work education of a substantial increase of ethnic minority group students and faculty and the development of curriculum more relevant to minority groups. One is immediately impressed by the fact that the three-pronged concern of CSWE cannot be isolated from the entire issue of racism and the battle against its manifestations in our country.[2]

Gradually, ethnic minority faculty were hired and special projects on the recruitment and training of ethnic minorities were funded by the federal government. Schools of social work initiated efforts to incorporate ethnic minority content into their curricula. CSWE's leadership in this area was evident in its appointment in 1970 of five ethnic minority task forces that were funded by the National Institute of Mental Health (NIMH). In 1973, the five task forces each published a report defining the issues and problems facing social work education in relation to their particular minority group.[3] The reports included recommendations about the recruitment of students and faculty members and the integration of ethnic minority content into the social work curriculum.

During the past fifteen years, CSWE has continued to provide leadership in this area through its Commission on Minority Groups. Two doctoral fellowship programs funded by NIMH in the research and clinical areas enabled CSWE to provide opportunities for ethnic minorities to develop leaders in these important fields.[4] CSWE also developed other projects, such as the Minority Faculty Development program and the Curriculum Project on Aging and Ethnic Minorities. The 1970s also were characterized by the funding of special ethnic-minority training and research centers for Hispanics, Asian Americans, blacks, and American Indians.

There is no doubt that during the decade of the 1970s, the National Association of Social Workers (NASW), as the only professional organization of social workers, also expressed its concern about ethnic minorities through its National Committee on Minority Affairs. However, it should be observed that despite the increase in the number of ethnic minority professional social workers, the ethnic minority membership of NASW remains low. Furthermore, during the 1970s, American Indians, blacks, Chicanos, Puerto Ricans, and Asian Americans organized their own associations of social workers.

The trends in social work education reviewed here developed during a period when the number of master's degree programs increased from 49 in 1950 to 89 in 1981. Doctoral programs quadrupled from 1960 to 1981, increasing from 15 in 1960 to 43 in 1981. In 1981, there were 301 accredited BSW programs. This growth in social work education was stimulated and supported by massive funding from the federal government.

TRENDS IN SOCIAL WORK EDUCATION FOR MINORITIES

What is the significance of the remarkable trend in the expansion of social work education for ethnic minorities? Has there been a great increase in the number of minority social workers serving their respective communities? Are faculties in schools of social work more knowledgeable about, competent in, and sensitive to the problems, issues, ideologies, concerns, and perspectives of ethnic minority populations? Has there been a systematic development and utilization in the social work curriculum of a body of knowledge about ethnic minority groups? Are current graduates of schools of social work competent in providing services to ethnic minority clients?

There is no question that the general trends in social work education just discussed have heightened the awareness of faculties in schools of social work and professionals in general about ethnic minority populations. Schools of social work, in their efforts to comply and respond to CSWE's Standard 1234A, have developed special courses on institutional racism and on topics related to the ethnic experience of blacks, Chicanos, American Indians, Asian Americans, and Puerto Ricans. Site-visit teams have attempted to apply this standard during their reviews of the accreditation status of schools of social work.

Writing about the conscious efforts made by schools of social work to alter their curricula to include minority issues, Leon stated the following:

> While these efforts have increased the presence of minority administrators, faculty and students, there is little indication that the curriculum, or the alteration of curriculum, has provided the knowledge, skills, and intervention strategies required to work effectively with minority people. There are indications that the incorporation of minority content into core curricula shows little sign of obtaining support or even becoming a reality.[5]

A cursory review of the enrollment of ethnic minority students in schools of social work during the last fifteen years indicates an increase in the number of such students, particularly from the mid-1960s to the mid-1970s. However, when the data on ethnic-oriented universities (Howard University for blacks and the University of Puerto Rico for Puerto Ricans) are adjusted for, it is found that the percentage of ethnic minorities who are receiving master's degrees has decreased since 1975. As Rubin noted, "the percentage of ethnic minority students enrolled in master's programs and receiving master's degrees appears relatively flat."[6] However, the CSWE statistical reports indicate a 3.2 percent drop per year from 1975 through 1981 in the number of master's degrees awarded to ethnic minorities. The baccalaureate programs remained steady in the number of ethnic minority students receiving BSW degrees: 27 percent. The reports also show a 24 percent reduction in financial aid from public sources to doctoral students, from 55.2 percent in 1978 to 31.2 percent in 1981 and a 12.1 percent reduction in financial aid to master's degree students, from 55.2 percent in 1978 to 43.1. Although financial aid from school and university sources increased 12.3 percent for MSW students and 26.1 percent for doctoral students, the net result was a significant reduction in financial aid for all students—particularly minority students. Williams stated the following:

> The mood in America has shifted from one favoring liberal reform and civil rights to one of political conservatism, retrenchment of civil rights, and racial backlash. As early as 1973, the Commission on Minority Groups of the Council on Social Work Education (CSWE) noted an alarming rise in conservatism among social work students. In research comparing the ideological stances of BSW and MSW students, Cyrns found a similar trend. It appears that the profession grows more conservative as the society does.[7]

Following the same theme, Koeske and Crouse's study concluded the following:

> Relative to Americans in general, and probably relative to those of similar age, income and education, the sociopolitical perspective of social work students and professionals is liberal. Our data suggests, however, that the liberal ideology of social workers may be *eroding* somewhat. [Emphasis added.]
>
> To some extent, therefore, social workers may be part of a conservative trend that analysts and ordinary citizens have perceived in the American population. . . .The implications of such a trend for social work practice, policy and education may be great.[8]

Since its inception, CSWE's Standard 1234A has aroused criticism and opposition from faculty members and administrators. At different times during the last decade, efforts have been made to clarify, limit, change, and even eliminate the standard. Its value and significance is attested to by CSWE's commitment to its maintenance and enforcement. Horner and Borrerro concluded that "the intent of the standard is clear and defenders argue, its utility manifest."[9] They found in interviews with site visitors that there is an inconsistency within and between schools in the application of the standard and that site visitors held the notion "that faculty and administrators frequently did not know how to incorporate minority content into the curriculum."[10] Furthermore, Schlesinger and Devore, in discussing the implications of their research, concluded:

> Those charged with the implementation of the CSWE's mandate concerning inclusion of materials on ethnic minority life must be aware of the persistent doubts raised (by ethnic minorities) about the validity of information conveyed and the qualifications of faculty who work in this arena....There is no doubt that efforts to increase minority faculty are essential.[11]

DEVELOPING AND USING A BODY OF KNOWLEDGE

Another critical issue has been the efforts that have been made to develop and use knowledge about ethnic minority groups in social work education. During the last two decades, a body of literature has emerged in the fields of psychology, sociology, anthropology, political science, economics, history, and education on such topics as racism, ethnic minorities of color, and the provision and utilization of social, health, and mental health services. As Schlesinger and Devore wrote:

> The apparent criticism of the behavioral sciences literature cannot be ignored. Reviewing this literature leaves little doubt that social work has made only a limited effort to develop its own body of knowledge— rather there is heavy reliance on sociological, psychological, and literary materials.[12]

In her review of the literature, Figueira-McDonough suggested that although the proliferation of articles on minorities, women, and the poor in the social work literature during the last two decades reflects the profession's concern, most of the articles have not gone beyond a statement of the problem, and the contention that social work has become more egalitarian lacks empirical support. She stated: "awareness of the problem has not been matched by systematic efforts to evaluate and respond to the problem [of discrimination] at the methodological and organizational levels."[13] In addition, in the May 1981 issue of *Social Work*, the editor-in-chief identified the need to develop knowledge about "oppressed people" that can be applied by the profession. She wrote:

> In order to do effective practice, more research is needed to determine in what specific situations and in what ways differences between workers and others in race, class, sex, and sexual orientation affect practice

activities. . . . Knowledge also is needed about the life experiences, culture, strengths, and history of specific groups. And knowledge is needed about effective and ineffective ways to deal with exploitation.[14]

A review of *Social Work* and the *Journal of Education for Social Work* revealed the following distribution of articles pertaining to ethnic minorities from January 1975 through December 1981. In the forty-two issues of *Social Work* from that period, five full-length articles were about blacks, five were about Chicanos, one was about Asian Americans, five were about American Indians, five were about the broad area of racism, three were related to discrimination, and three were on cross-cultural practice; none were on Puerto Ricans. The November 1979 "Special Issue on Family Policy" carried only one article on ethnic minorities. The most important issue of *Social Work* was the special issue on "Social Work and People of Color," which included material on all ethnic minorities. During the same period, the twenty-one issues of *Journal of Education for Social Work* included four articles on blacks; none on Chicanos, Asian Americans, American Indians, or Puerto Ricans; and thirteen in general areas related to ethnic minorities.

It is important to note that in the early 1970s, the Western Interstate Commission on Higher Education (WICHE), with funding from NIMH, developed a curriculum project that produced about fifteen monographs that specifically addressed each area of the social work curriculum in terms of specific ethnic minority groups. WICHE also sponsored a conference and published a monograph entitled *Research: A Third World Perspective*.[15] CSWE sponsored a similar conference and published another monograph. Other reports, papers, and monographs emerged from the fifteen ethnic minority social work training projects funded by NIMH. The Chicano Training Center (Houston, Texas), Worden School of Social Service (Our Lady of the Lake University, San Antonio, Texas), Asian-American Mental Health Training Center (Los Angeles), Arizona State University School of Social Work (Tempe), University of Utah School of Social Work (Salt Lake City), California State University (San Jose), and other programs were part of this effort.

In sum, although ethnic minority authors have made important and timely contributions to knowledge about their particular population, the professional publications have paid limited attention to them. There continues to be a wide gap between the development of a systematic body of knowledge and its integration into the social work curriculum and the fields of practice.

There is no doubt that a serious effort has been made to develop ethnic-specific knowledge in social work education. However, the utilization of this knowledge is still the most important task needed in training competent social workers for practice in minority communities. The transition from making knowledge available to applying it in the classroom and field practicum remains a pedagogical challenge for social work educators. Furthermore, the development of social work knowledge through research on practice with ethnic minorities is an uncharted field.

SOCIAL SERVICES IN MINORITY COMMUNITIES

During the decade of the civil rights movement and the Great Society (1962–72), the hopes and aspirations of ethnic minorities increased in proportion to the positive cues these groups received from the establishment. The Great Society became a goal of the War on Poverty and civil rights legislation. Concepts such as "maximum feasible participation" and "new careers for the poor" became the symbols of action against racism and oppression in the land of plenty. At the same time, indigenous leaders in minority communities were talking about "empowerment," "community control," "self-determination," and "indigenous social services."

The experiment of the Great Society and the civil rights movement provided a renewed hope and impetus for the development of social services controlled by ethnic groups in their communities. The social work profession and schools of social work reacted to these movements rather than responding with a planned proactive approach. As in the Progressive Era, "social work took an aggressive and positive stance toward social change."[16] However, as the Great Society programs became politicized and ethnic minorities learned to use them as an effective community and political action tool, the federal government saw the need to protect its status quo by emasculating the War on Poverty. The support for "maximum feasible participation" and "community control" was

> . . .quickly withdrawn as it became evident that federal funds were being utilized for organizing efforts to challenge public institutions. As public support diminished, social work did not hold to its tenuous commitment to community organization. [Rather, the profession settled for a] seemingly more technologically advanced planning methodology, a more politically acceptable administrative focus, or a more passive service delivery system.[17]

Today, more than ever before, it is important to question whether the social work profession and the social welfare establishment are servants or masters of minority communities. This statement should be understood within the context of the social control functions of the profession and the public and private social welfare systems. It should also be understood in relation to the concept of self-determination and its glaring absence in the relationship between ethnic minorities and the social welfare establishment.

As in the late 1940s and the Nixon era of the late 1960s, in this era of Reaganomics, the social work profession is manifesting its characteristic ambivalence about its commitment to social change. As Stewart stated:

> The percentage of social workers in the country who are directly involved professionally with the poor and with disadvantaged populations has steadily declined; social work by and large serves the middle class of our society. Within the framework of the social work principle of "self determination," who then are the real clients of social workers? Should social workers allow these *real* clients to determine what they need and want from social work?[18]

And, as Longres pointed out:

> Social work has, to some extent justifiably, been criticized as an instrument of conservative politics. Certainly, some aspects of the profession and the individuals involved in it suggest that more concern will always be given to controlling the ambition of minorities than to reducing the domination of the majority. Those who provide social services. are beholden to the majority because these services derive legitimacy and funding from them. Services exist to the extent that the more affluent and powerful are willing to mandate them and support them through taxes and philanthropic contributions. Furthermore, social workers have been traditionally drawn from the ranks of the majority or from upwardly mobile groups that have used the majority as a reference point. It is thus more likely that social control will define the general parameters of service delivery.[19]

SOCIOPOLITICAL PERSPECTIVE

The profession's ambivalence about its role and commitment to social change is becoming more evident as social workers struggle for recognition, professional status, and legitimization by the society. These professional goals were achieved to some extent through the extensive funding of public programs as the welfare state evolved from the New Deal of the 1930s to the Great Society of the 1960s.

No other factor contributed more to the remarkable development of social work education and the profession than the funding of public programs at the federal and state governmental levels. However, it is ironic to observe that these resources have been viewed as a shining hope for the eradication of poverty; social, political, and economic injustice; and discrimination both for the profession and the people it is supposed to serve. Social work has become, to some extent, subservient to the public sector; it has placed its practice emphasis, as Longres suggested, on the safe arena of personal troubles and services and has deemphasized the critical issues of cultural subordination and racial inequality. Public programs that have been funded during the past thirty years and which made employment possible (directly or indirectly) for the majority of professional social workers represented a unique opportunity for the empowerment and liberation of the people social workers are supposed to serve.

Social work cannot be practiced outside the environmental context. That is, a fundamental sociopolitical context, particularly as it applies to ethnic minorities, is inherent in social work practice. Longres posed the following challenge to the profession:

> We may either stand in favor of minorities, encouraging their collective self-determination and facilitating their attempts to alter the status of their communities, or we may come down on the side of the majority and aid in the maintenance of its dominion. If we choose to work in behalf of minorities, practice and service must be defined to include social reform activities.[20]

CONCLUSION

In the absence of significant efforts by social workers (both minority and majority) to implement strategies of empowerment in minority communities, the conservative mood of this decade will emerge as a dominant force to reshape professional practice as a greater agent of social control. Social work education for ethnic minorities seems to be moving in this direction. Although important gains have been made, particularly in the last decade, the dependence on federal funds for the provision of fellowships and financial aid and for the hiring of ethnic minority faculty members through federally funded projects will undoubtedly result in the following:

1. The drop in enrollment of ethnic minority students during the last six years will become more evident in 1984 when most

if not all the federal training funds will be eliminated. Although there has been an increase in financial aid provided by schools and universities, given the state of the economy, the loss of federal funding will not be replaced.

2. The number of minority faculty members will decrease or at best remain at the current level.

3. Efforts to develop and use minority-specific curricula and knowledge also will be reduced or hampered by the loss of funding and the shifting of priorities stimulated by the conservative trend.

4. Research on issues, concerns, problems, policies, and services in relation to ethnic minorities will decrease or will be deemphasized.

5. The training of social workers may increasingly be focused on or directed toward personal, psychological, and pathological problems, and less emphasis will be placed on environmental and institutional factors.

Other critical situations may have an impact on these trends and may change their direction. The most significant of them are the high unemployment rate among ethnic minority youths (35–40 percent); the growing dissatisfaction, disillusionment, and conflict over limited resources and broken promises among minorities; and better-prepared ethnic minority leaders. These situations may create the ferment and action necessary to elicit a more responsible approach from schools of social work, the social welfare establishment, and, particularly, the federal government.

Ethnic minorities of color cannot and will not become another statistical trend in the evolution of social work education. They have become and will continue to be in the mainstream of social work education. Conflict over limited resources for jobs, good schools, income maintenance, health care, better housing, and college and professional education has been the trend in the lives of ethnic minorities because their legitimate access to them has always been denied.

Notes and References

1. Statistics presented in this paper are based on the annual statistical reports of the Council on Social Work Education (*Statistics on Social Work Education in the United States, 1975–81*).

2. As quoted in G. M. Styles O'Neal and C. A. Scott, *Supplying a Critical Need: Preparing Ethnic Minority Doctoral Social Work Students for Leadership* (New York: Council on Social Work Education, 1981), p. 18.

3. Juliette Ruiz, ed., *Chicano Task Force Report*, E. Aracelis Francis, ed., *Black Task Force Report: Suggested Guides for the Integration of Black Content into*

the Social Work Curriculum, Kenji Murasi, ed., *Asian American Task Force Report: Problems and Issues in Social Work Education,* and Magdalena Miranda, ed., *Puerto Rican Task Force Report* (New York: Council on Social Work Education, all 1973).

4. O'Neal and Scott, *Supplying a Critical Need.* (The Minority Research Doctoral Fellowship Program was initiated in 1974, and the Minority Clinical Doctoral Fellowship Program, in 1978).

5. Edwina Leon, "The Melting Pot Fable: Achieving Effective Social Work Practice with Minorities of Color." Unpublished manuscript, California, 1981, p. 16.

6. Allen Rubin, *Statistics on Social Work Education in the United States: 1981* (New York: Council on Social Work Education, 1982).

7. Leon F. Williams, "Measuring Racism: An Example from Education," *Social Work,* 27 (January 1982), p. 111.

8. Gary F. Koeske and Mary A. Crouse, "Liberalism-Conservatism in Samples of Social Work Students and Professionals," *Social Service Review,* 55 (June 1961), pp. 193–205.

9. William Horner and Michael Borrerro, "A Planning Matrix for Standard 1234A," *Journal of Education for Social Work,* 17 (Winter 1982), pp. 36–43.

10. Ibid., p. 40.

11. Elfriede G. Schlesinger and Wynetta Devore, "Social Workers View Ethnic Minority Teaching," *Journal of Education for Social Work,* 15 (Fall 1979), p. 26.

12. Ibid.

13. Josefina Figueira-McDonough, "Discrimination in Social Work: Evidence, Myth, and Ignorance," *Social Work,* 24 (May 1979), p. 221.

14. Anne Minahan, "Social Workers and Oppressed People," Editorial, *Social Work,* 26 (May 1981), p. 184.

15. *Research: A Third World Perspective* (Boulder, Colo.: Western Interstate Commission for Higher Education, January 1976).

16. Jeffrey Galper and Jacqueline Mondros, "Community Organization in the 1980's: Fact or Fiction," *Journal of Education for Social Work,* 16 (Winter 1980), p. 42.

17. Ibid., pp. 42–43.

18. Robert P. Stewart, "Watershed Days: How Will Social Work Respond to the Conservative Revolution?" *Social Work,* 26 (July 1981), p. 271.

19. John F. Longres, "Minority Groups: An Interest-Group Perspective," *Social Work,* 27 (January 1982), p. 12.

20. Ibid.

Conflicts and Coping Strategies of Minority Female Graduate Students

Jewelle Taylor Gibbs

In 1970, the Center for Research and Development in Higher Education at the University of California at Berkeley published a collection of essays entitled *The Minority Student on the Campus: Expectations and Possibilities*.[1] These essays provided a comprehensive and well-documented overview of the accommodation of minority students to predominantly white universities. As Hodgkinson asserted, "minority group member plus student equals subordination squared."[2] Hodgkinson meant that minority students experience double repression because they are both students and members of a minority group.

None of the essays in that collection dealt specifically with a subgroup of the minority student population: female graduate students. Thus, the question remains: How does the status of being female further contribute to the subordination or repression experienced by minority students in graduate school? As Ison-Franklin pointed out:

> If one considers that, within the United States, personal value is highest for the white male, then being minority and female constitutes a special handicap with respect to acceptability in the prestigious institutions and professions. Mechanisms for coping with an exclusionary system which discounts one's net worth on both these criteria require an extraordinary personal effort.[3]

This article identifies some of the sources of stress and psychological conflicts experienced by minority women in their roles as graduate students in predominantly white universities and describes the strategies they use to cope with these conflicts. The data that form the basis for this analysis were derived from the author's experience as a clinical social worker at a private university mental health clinic in the San Francisco Bay Area.

REVIEW OF THE LITERATURE

Several authors have commented on the dearth of research on the educational and occupational aspirations of minority women, particularly since the civil rights movement of the late 1960s presumably had a significant impact on the way these women perceive themselves and their opportunities.[4] Although it is apparent that women, in general, experience stress when they enter male-dominated professional programs in graduate schools, little information is available that distinguishes the experiences of majority and minority women.[5]

Four areas of the empirical and clinical literature are relevant to this topic: the fear of success by female college students, sex-role attitudes and stereotyping in this group, role conflicts in married college women, and stresses experienced by women in graduate training programs. These areas will be discussed next.

Fear of success. Horner's well-known finding that female undergraduates exhibited fear and avoidance of success has frequently been replicated in samples of white college women.[6] Although Weston and Mednick's 1969 study found that black women scored significantly lower than did white women on their level of fear of success, a replication of that study in 1971 did not support the finding of racial differences, primarily because the white women showed significantly lower levels of the fear of success than did the white women in the previous study.[7] Empirical studies of this type of fear in other minority women college students have not been cited in the literature.

Sex-role attitudes and stereotyping. Maccoby and Jacklin's review of the studies in this area confirmed the consistent finding that men and women share similar attitudes toward appropriate sex-role behaviors for boys and girls.[8] These attitudes are reinforced by socialization practices, social-role expectations, and the mass media. However, recent studies have shown that black women view nontraditional roles as equally appropriate for them as for men[9] and that women who occupy nontraditional roles are psychologically healthier than women in traditional roles.[10] Carillo suggested that the "rigid adherence to sex-roles and gender-appropriate behavior" is rapidly changing among Hispanics [and is thus] allowing women greater personal and economic independence.[11]

Role conflicts. The few studies of the impact of marital status on female graduate students suggest that women experience a conflict between their roles as wives and their roles as students.[12] In a national survey of graduate students, Feldman found that married female students were more likely than their male counterparts to be older, to be enrolled part time, to have fewer articles published, to interact less with fellow students, and to be more family oriented.[13] In addition, she found that single and married women were more likely than men to feel that they might have to withdraw from graduate school because of emotional strain.

Stresses in professional training. Studies of women in graduate programs primarily have been clinical and descriptive. Reports of women in medical school have consistently noted that women experience stress because of competition with male students, the lack of role models, and the lack of mentor relationships.[14] In integrated medical schools, black female medical students tend to attribute the stress they experience more to their race and, in predominantly black medical schools, they attribute it to their sex.[15] In a clinical study of black female graduate students, Gibbs found that these women most frequently reported marital, academic, financial, and role-conflict problems.[16]

Theoretical Model

In his analysis of the role behavior of college-educated married women, Hall developed a model of coping with role conflict that is based on concepts from role theory, ego psychology, and organizational behavior.[17] He suggested that women experience greater role conflict than do men from the demands of multiple roles. Hall identified sixteen types of coping strategies, grouped into three broad areas—structural-role definition, personal-role definition, and reactive-role behavior. Structural-role definition (Type 1) involves the alteration of externally imposed expectations of a woman's structural position. Personal-role definition (Type 2) involves the changing of one's expectations and perceptions of a given position. Reactive-role behavior (Type 3) involves efforts to meet all role expectations.

This model is useful in analyzing the role behavior of female minority graduate students who must assume many different roles in various contexts. It also is useful to view the behavior of these women in a cross-cultural perspective, which posits that ethnic minorities, because of their relatively disadvantaged status in American society, have developed similar attitudes and strategies in their attempts to cope with the dominant society.[18] The implications of these models for prevention and clinical intervention for the special needs of this group of minority women will be discussed next.

CLINICAL DATA

Forty-six female graduate students of ethnic minority backgrounds were seen by the author for individual or group counseling over a period of five years at a student health center at a private university in the San Francisco Bay Area, where she worked as a clinical social worker from 1970 to 1974 and from 1978 to 1979. The forty-six women included twenty-six who were black, fourteen who were Hispanic, four who were Native American, and two who were Japanese American. They were enrolled in a variety of graduate training programs, including education, law, medicine, and the social sciences. The women ranged in age from 21 to 35 ($\overline{X}$ = 25) and represented a broad diversity of socioeconomic and geographic backgrounds. Eight were married, four were divorced, and thirty-four were single. Five of the women had children, but two of them were single mothers. Although the majority described themselves as middle class, twelve women described their family backgrounds as "working class" or "blue collar." Case examples drawn from case records of and interviews with these women will be used to illustrate the sources of their stress, the nature of their conflicts, and the coping strategies they used to resolve their conflicts. The identifying characteristics of the cases have been altered to protect the identities of the clients.

Stresses and Conflicts

The four sources of stress most frequently mentioned by the women in counseling sessions were academic stress, competing demands from family and community, male-female relationships, and the choice of a career. The married graduate students had a fifth source of stress—the complexity of juggling the roles of wife, student, and, sometimes, mother. These sources of stress can be viewed as precursors of psychological conflicts and can be conceptualized in five major dimensions: performance, autonomy, intimacy, commitment, and identity; they are summarized in Table 1, p. 39.

Academic stress. Academic stress may have increased for minority graduate students in the past ten years as a result of the debate over affirmative action. Even though a minority woman can obviously be considered to fill two "quotas," she often is perceived as a case of "special admission" without equal qualifications. Moreover, she frequently is excluded from research opportunities and other preprofessional activities that would enhance her training and lead to the most desirable jobs.

This source of stress is related to a conflict in the area of performance; that is, many minority female graduate students experience severe conflict in their efforts to demonstrate their competence to their professors and peers. This conflict may express itself in heightened tension in academic situations, inability to concentrate on studies, procrastination in completing assignments, the lack of motivation to complete requirements for a degree, and a general fear of failure. The following case study illustrates this conflict:

> Justine, a 23-year-old graduate student, was reared in Arizona as the middle child of a white skilled worker and his Navajo wife. When she was 11, the family moved to Los Angeles, where she experienced culture shock after a childhood in a predominantly American Indian community. After an excellent record in high school and a state college, she won a graduate fellowship to the university, where she experienced another period of culture shock. She complained that her professors expected her to be an expert on American Indian culture, but treated her condescendingly and had low expectations of her academic potential. She responded to these messages by studying constantly, refusing to participate in American Indian support groups, and avoiding social life. By the end of the winter quarter, she had become fatigued and irritable and was unable to concentrate on her work or complete her term assignments. She sought counseling because she was beginning to question her abilities and competence and to fear that she could not survive in such a nonsupportive and competitive environment.

Family-community demands. A second major source of stress is the family's and community's competition for the time of the minority female student. Minority students frequently come from extended families that place a higher premium on kinship networks and cooperation than on individuality and autonomy, particularly for women; therefore, the women often feel conflicted about fulfilling their family obligations and their study assignments.[19] Similarly, minority students may want to participate in community activities as a way of maintaining their cultural identity while in graduate school. Obviously, these two sets of demands from family and community are usually incompatible with the schedules and pressures of graduate training, and thus many students experience severe psychological conflict.

This source of stress is related to a conflict in the area of autonomy; many female minority students report feeling conflicted in their attempts to balance the academic demands of graduate school with the competing demands from their family and community networks. This conflict may express itself in ambivalence toward one or both sets of pressures, defensiveness or overprotective feelings toward one's family or community obligations, overinvolvement in community activities, or withdrawal from and rejection of family and community networks. It is demonstrated in the case study of Anna:

Anna, a 25-year-old Chicano from Southern California, was a third-year student in the health sciences. As the eldest of six children in a traditional Mexican-American family, she was often called home to participate in holidays and to settle family disputes. In addition, she was active in MECHA and served as a recruiter of and student adviser for other Hispanic students in her program. Since she had acquired a reputation as an effective organizer and dynamic speaker, she often was invited to speak at community festivals and student conferences. Gradually, her academic work deteriorated, and her instructors began to criticize her clinical work. Her family obligations escalated when her parents separated and she was unable to fulfill all her extracurricular commitments. Anna began to express ambivalence toward her family and refused to answer calls and letters asking for her help. She also withdrew from several community activities, but felt guilty about disappointing her friends. These feelings of guilt made her feel depressed, and she found herself constantly apologizing for not meeting all her obligations. Finally, she sought counseling when her feelings of alienation and despair made it difficult for her to carry out her academic tasks.

Male-female relationships. The third major source of stress is the redefinition of male-female relationships. Although the women's liberation movement has had the most visible impact on a reexamination of male-female relationships in the wider society, the civil rights movement had a curious counterbalancing effect on the relationship between minority men and women.[20]

Many minority women are confused about where their own best interests lie—whether they should subordinate their own career interests and goals to those of their lovers or husbands. While minority women are seeking better educational and occupational opportunities so that their working lives will be both more stimulating and more financially rewarding, minority men are trying to improve their economic position and to establish their ability to support their families as de facto heads of their households. Although these goals can be viewed as complementary, minority men sometimes perceive the women's ambition and assertiveness as too threatening to their own sense of competence and self-esteem.[21] The men's perceptions inevitably create anxiety among minority women, problems of communication between men and women, and discrepancies between their mutual goals and aspirations.

This source of stress is related to conflicts in the area of intimacy. The stress in male-female relationships causes minority women to feel conflicted about the most effective ways to establish relationships (intimacy) with those minority men whom they perceive as appropriate marital choices. The women express this conflict by their anxiety about reinforcing negative female stereotypes, hostility toward minority men for dating white women, fears of rejection, and an unwillingness to commit themselves to an exclusive relationship. The case of Gladys illustrates this point:

> Gladys, a 26-year-old black woman from the South, was in her final year of doctoral studies in a social science field. Both her parents were professionals, and she had attended a predominantly black college with conservative traditions. Her initial adjustment to graduate school had been difficult, but her academic difficulties had been overshadowed by her social problems. She had experienced several unsatisfactory affairs with black male colleagues, as well as subtle forms of sexual harassment from several of her professors. Her background did not prepare her for the casual attitudes toward sex, interracial dating, and the shared households of unmarried couples. She was constantly teased by her friends about her puritanical "square" views, yet she was unwilling to change her behavior. When she ended her last relationship (with a male doctoral student), he accused her of being an aggressive, emasculating female who put her own career goals before their relationship. Yet this same man had refused to make a long-term commitment to her and continued to date other women. This series of abortive relationships caused her to feel depressed about ever establishing a mutually rewarding relationship and to question her femininity and sexuality. A friend referred her for counseling after she noted that Gladys was becoming increasingly alienated from her male friends, expressing hostility toward all interracial couples, and threatening to drop out of school.

Career choice. A fourth major source of stress is the choice of a career goal—how to use one's professional training most effectively. Should the minority female student select a position in the private sector or in the public sector? Since minority students frequently are in debt when they complete their education, positions in the private sector naturally attract them. Yet, many of these women are committed to returning to their communities to provide professional, technical, and managerial services to depressed urban economies.

This source of stress is related to conflicts in the area of commitment—conflicts about such priorities as individual versus group needs, personal advancement versus community service, high income and status versus moderate income and service, and breaking down barriers in nontraditional fields versus strengthening resources in minority communities. The following case study of Maria shows these conflicts:

> Maria, a 25-year-old Chicana from New Mexico, was in her last year of law school. As an undergraduate, Maria had been active in MECHA and was recruited to law school through a special minority recruitment drive. Although she was interested in joining the farm labor movement, her studies prevented her from participating in many activist causes. Her ambivalence toward her studies was further exacerbated by a summer internship in an agency that provided legal services to low-income *barrio* residents. When she returned to school for her second year, she became involved in a research project in which she could combine her interests in labor law and the rights of low-income workers. Her enthusiasm and competence as a researcher made her attractive to a variety of law firms when she was interviewing for jobs in the fall of her third year. She felt strongly that her advocacy skills were needed to improve legal services for low-income Chicanos. Yet, she was excited by the prospect of obtaining a challenging position in a corporate law firm where she would be breaking down barriers and learning valuable skills. She sought counseling when she became increasingly anxious about the job interviews and began to feel indecisive about her personal and professional priorities.

Role complexity. The special case of the married graduate student with children provides an example of a fifth source of stress—role complexity. Marriage per se adds another role and another dimension to the graduate student's life. It can be more stressful or less stressful, depending on whether the husband is a student or a wage earner, whether the wife and husband have a satisfactory division of labor in their home, and whether they have mutual goals and aspirations for their careers. However stressful the marital relationship, the wife-student can deal with her husband as another adult who is able to manage his own life. Such is not the case with dependent children. The student-mother who has to work out child care arrangements, monitor the child's psychosocial and health needs, and participate in the child's school and recreational activities often must place the needs of her child before her own needs as a student, particularly when the child is ill or when child care arrangements break down. All these stresses are exacerbated for those graduate students who are single mothers without regular partners.

This source of stress is related to a conflict in the area of personal identity; that is minority female graduate students who are wives and mothers have difficulty maintaining a sense of balance in their personal identities because of conflicting expectations and demands from their multiple roles. They feel resentment toward their husbands for not giving them sufficient empathy or support, frustration because they do not have enough time to spend with their families, and exhausted and depressed from their role overload. The case study of Paula illustrates these conflicts:

> Paula, a 27-year-old graduate student, was reared in the Midwest as the eldest daughter of a middle-class black family. She returned to graduate school four years after marrying her college sweetheart, who was employed in an electronics firm. They had a three-year-old child who was enrolled in an all-day nursery school while both parents pursued their goals. Paula maintained a busy schedule that required her to be organized and efficient, particularly because she prided herself on being a superachiever. In addition to a demanding graduate program, she frequently entertained her husband's colleagues or accompanied him to company functions, volunteered as an aide once a week in her daughter's nursery school, and participated actively in the black graduate student association. She began to suffer migraine headaches and experienced sudden outbursts of crying whenever her schedule was disrupted in any way, and she began to worry that her professors would perceive her work as below the quality of the other students. Early in the spring quarter, she sought counseling to help her deal with the stresses of her multiple roles because she felt she could no longer be "all things to all people."

These five sources of stress are the major ones that the sample of minority female graduate students identified in counseling sessions. Most women complained of multiple stresses and conflicts ($\overline{X} = 2.9$), but usually perceived one source of stress as the major problem. They exhibited a number of symptoms in dealing with these single or multiple stresses, ranging from anxiety and depres-

Table 1.

Adaptive and Maladaptive Coping Strategies for Dealing with Sources of Stress

Sources of Stress	Dimensions of Psychological Conflict	Coping Strategies	
		Adaptive	Maladaptive
Academic pressures	Performance	Demonstrating competence	Overachievement syndrome
Family and community commitments	Autonomy	Setting priorities	Overinvolvement syndrome
Male-female relationships	Intimacy	Risk taking	Disengagement syndrome
Career options	Commitment	Utilizing resources	Immobilization syndrome
Role complexity	Identity	Negotiating role limits	Superwoman syndrome

sion to psychosomatic symptoms and hysterical conversion symptoms. Although some women developed a number of symptoms, others developed coping strategies to handle the stresses that seemed to have a cumulative effect on their psyches.

The various coping strategies utilized by the women in the sample are described next. It is important to note that each woman developed a predominant coping strategy designed to handle her major source of stress, but coping strategies also were used in combination and often overlapped.

COPING STRATEGIES

The coping strategy chosen by minority female graduate students to handle stress depends on a number of factors, such as learned family and cultural patterns, personality attributes, previous methods of dealing with stress, use of support systems, and perceptions of alternatives in the environment. Some strategies were more adaptive than others toward the goal of obtaining a graduate education. Although other strategies may have temporarily alleviated symptoms and given the student some feelings of satisfaction, they were ultimately counterproductive and dysfunctional in the university environment (see Table 1).

First, those who experienced conflicts in performance owing to academic stress utilized the *overachievement syndrome* in which they worked hard academically and neglected their personal, social, and recreational needs to demonstrate to the faculty and fellow students that they were intellectually competent. This strategy was maladaptive because it often resulted in burnout. These students became fatigued and irritable and were unable to function effectively. This strategy fits Hall's definition of reactive role behavior.[22]

Second, those women who experienced conflicts in autonomy, generated by pressures from their families and communities to maintain close ties, frequently exhibited an *overinvolvement syndrome.* This coping strategy was maladaptive because it resulted in a dual set of commitments that often were in conflict and which fostered a constant double-bind for the students. Frequently, it caused them to feel ambivalent toward the demands of their family and community and lessened their ability to carry out academic assignments. This strategy can also be categorized as reactive role behavior.

Third, those women who experienced conflicts in intimacy because of conflicts in their heterosexual relationships, frequently reported using the coping strategy of a *disengagement syndrome.* Several women stated that it was least painful to avoid relationships with men and to act indifferent and even hostile so they would not face sexual exploitation, humiliation, or rejection. This strategy was maladaptive for establishing healthy heterosexual relationships and was far from satisfactory in view of their stated intention of finding a suitable mate. It can be viewed as personal role redefinition, according to Hall's model.[23]

Fourth, those women who experienced conflicts of commitment from their increased career options, used a coping strategy that can be best described as the *immobilization syndrome.* This strategy was characterized by increased anxiety about seeking a job as they neared completion of their degree requirements, feelings of defensiveness about any desire for personal benefits or advancement in a career, and procrastination about committing themselves to a specific job or deciding among several job offers. While many women recognized that their race and sex had given them a slight advantage for obtaining some positions, they often were reluctant to press this advantage. Sometimes they deliberately sabotaged their opportunities for a prestigious entry-level position by arriving late for interviews; dressing, speaking, or behaving inappropriately; or neglecting to follow up on inquiries from potential employers. Again, this strategy involved a personal role redefinition.

Fifth, those women (especially married women and single mothers) who experienced conflicts of personal identity generated by the stress of role complexity frequently reported using the coping strategy that can be called the *superwoman syndrome*. With this strategy, the students attempted to organize every aspect of their lives so they could adequately fulfill the roles of wife-mother-student. In trying to juggle all of these tasks, many women developed a number of obsessive-compulsive patterns and rigid schedules. However, when there were unanticipated disruptions, their anxiety about losing control of their highly structured life resulted in psychosomatic symptoms, insomnia, or other disabling behaviors. This strategy represented another form of reactive role behavior.

Although white female graduate students also adopt these maladaptive coping strategies, the author believes that these strategies tend to be exacerbated among minority women students. That is, these strategies are more threatening to the mental health of minority women because they are inextricably tied to the women's perceptions of their abilities and competence and of how their professors and fellow students view them.

INTERVENTION STRATEGIES

How can mental health professionals effectively intervene with female minority students who seek counseling for any of these conflicts? First, it is important that they should be knowledgeable about and sensitive to the particular pressures these students experience because of their ethnic and sociocultural backgrounds. Professionals can gain such knowledge by attending classes and workshop presentations on the range of cultural beliefs, values, and behaviors of the major ethnic groups in the local university population; by participating in case conferences that focus on cross-cultural issues; and by reading evaluative research on the effectiveness of various forms of treatment with minority clients.[24]

Second, mental health professionals can help these clients develop more appropriate and adaptive coping strategies for the conflicts described. The alternative positive strategies that can be used to deal with each type of conflict are schematically outlined in Table 1. These strategies are viewed as examples of structural role redefinition in that they alter a woman's external, structurally imposed expectations. Utilizing an ego-supportive approach, the author focused on helping these clients to identify their conflicts, to evaluate their behavioral consequences, and to work out the following coping behaviors that reduced their anxieties and promoted positive functioning:

■ The women who reported a conflict in performance were helped to assess their abilities realistically, to enhance their self-esteem, and to demonstrate their competence in appropriate competitive behaviors without becoming involved in a compensatory overachievement strategy.

■ The women who reported a conflict in autonomy were helped to gain a more realistic perspective on their obligations toward their family and community, to set priorities on the deployment of their time and energy, and to work out their feelings of ambivalence toward both sets of priorities. By reordering their priorities and forming substitute social networks in the academic community, they were able to avoid the pitfalls of overinvolvement in and overcommitment to the nonacademic spheres of their lives.

■ The women who reported a conflict in intimacy were helped to examine their attitudes toward and expectations of heterosexual relationships, to evaluate their sexual and social needs and preferences, and to accept risk taking as an important element in establishing trust and openness in a relationship. By fostering an attitude of self-appraisal and openness to new social experiences, the author helped these students move toward a strategy of engagement rather than disengagement in male-female relationships.

■ The women who reported a conflict in professional commitments, precipitated by the stress generated by increased career options for minority women, were helped to distinguish between their personal interests and goals and the collective needs and goals of their ethnic communities, to focus on a flexible graduate program that would enable them to maximize their professional options, and to establish an apprenticeship relationship with a professor who would serve as a mentor to facilitate their professional development. Thus, they were able to replace the dysfunctional strategy of immobilization with the more adaptive coping strategy of flexibility and utilization of the mentor-student relationship.

■ The women who experienced a conflict in personal identity, exacerbated by the complexity of playing multiple roles as graduate students, wives, and mothers, were helped to analyze the essential components of each role, to establish boundaries around the demands of each role, and to negotiate with husbands and children to distribute household responsibilities more equitably. Thus, they were able to substitute the more adaptive coping strategy of negotiation to delimit roles and to redistribute tasks for the less adaptive superwoman syndrome.

Third, mental health professionals should offer opportunities for mental health consultation to faculty, administrative staff, and other groups in the university community, as well as to allied professionals in the surrounding local communities. More and more mature women are entering college and graduate school, and an increasing number of them are from minority groups whose world views, experiences, and problems are different from those of the dominant group. This accelerating trend in higher education requires that mental health professionals provide objective information to their academic colleagues about the diverse cultural backgrounds of these women so that problems in cross-cultural communication can be anticipated, a greater sensitivity to these women's values and customs can be fostered, and adequate supportive services and networks to facilitate their successful adaptation to the university environment can be developed.

Notes and References

1. R. Altman and P. Snyder, eds., *The Minority Student on the Campus: Expectations and Possibilities* (Berkeley, Calif.: Center for Research and Development in Higher Education, University of California, 1970).

2. H. Hodgkinson, "Subordination Squared—The Minority Student," in ibid., p. 252.

3. Eleanor Ison-Franklin, "The Black Woman Medical Student in a Predominantly Black Professional School." Proceedings of the conference on *The Minority Woman in America: Professionalism at What Cost?* (San Francisco: Program for Women in Health Sciences, University of California, 1979), p. 30.

4. See, for example, Toni Cade, *The Black Woman: An Anthology* (New York: New American Library, 1974); J. Griscom, "Sex, Race and Class: Three Dimensions of Women's Experience," and J. Helms, "Black Women," *Counseling Psychologist*, 8 (January 1979), pp. 10-11 and 40-41, respectively.

5. Saul D. Feldman, "Impediment or Stimulant: Marital Status and Graduate Education," *American Journal of Sociology*, 78 (1973), pp. 982-994.

6. Matina Horner, "Toward an Understanding of Achievement Related Conflicts in Women," in Martha T. Mednick, Sandra Tangri, and Lois Hoffman, eds., *Women and Achievement: Social and Motivational Analyses* (New York: John Wiley & Sons, 1975), pp. 206-220.

7. Peter J. Weston and Martha T. Mednick, "Race, Social Class and the Motive to Avoid Success in Women," *Journal of Cross-Cultural Psychology*, 1 (September 1970), pp. 283-291; and Mednick and Gwendolyn R. Puryear, "Race and Fear of Success in College Women: 1968 and 1971," *Journal of Consulting and Clinical Psychology*, 44 (October 1976), pp. 787-789.

8. Eleanor E. Maccoby and Carol N. Jacklin, *The Psychology of Sex Differences* (Stanford, Calif.: Stanford University Press, 1976).

9. H. Farmer, "What Inhibits Achievement and Career Motivation in Women?" *Counseling Psychologist*, 6 (April 1976), pp. 12-14.

10. L. Oliver, "Counseling Implications of Recent Research on Women," *Personnel and Guidance Journal*, 53 (1975), pp. 430–437.

11. Carmen Carillo, "Changing Norms of Hispanic Families: Implications for Treatment," in Enrico E. Jones and Sheldon J. Korchin, eds., *Minority Mental Health* (New York: Praeger Publishers, 1982), p. 255.

12. See, for example, Feldman, "Impediment or Stimulant"; and Louise F. Fitzgerald and John O. Crites, "Toward a Career Psychology of Women: What Do We Know? What Do We Need to Know?" *Journal of Counseling Psychology*, 27 (January 1980), pp. 44–62.

13. Feldman, "Impediment or Stimulant."

14. See, for example, V. Davidson, "Coping Styles of Women Medical Students," *Journal of Medical Education*, 53 (1978), pp. 902–907; and M. Goldstein, "Preventive Mental Health Efforts for Women Medical Students," *Journal of Medical Education*, 50 (1975), pp. 289–291.

15. See, for example, Paul Guillory, "Black Medical Students Under Stress," unpublished master's degree thesis, California State University at Hayward, 1979; and Ison-Franklin, "The Black Woman Medical Student in a Predominantly Black Professional School."

16. Jewelle Taylor Gibbs, "Use of Mental Health Services by Black Students at a Predominantly White University: A Three-Year Study," *American Journal of Orthopsychiatry*, 45 (April 1975), pp. 430–445.

17. Douglas T. Hall, "A Model of Coping with Role Conflict: The Role Behavior of College Educated Women," *Administrative Science Quarterly*, 17 (December 1972), pp. 471–486.

18. Jones and Korchin, eds., *Minority Mental Health*.

19. See, for example, Carol B. Stack, *All Our Kin: Strategies for Survival in a Black Community* (New York: Harper & Row, 1974).

20. B. Johnson, "Ethnic Minority Feminism: A Minority Member's View," *Journal of the National Association of Women Deans and Counselors*, 41 (1978), pp. 52–55.

21. Robert Staples, *The World of Black Singles: Changing Patterns of Male/Female Relations* (Westport, Conn.: Greenwood Press, 1981).

22. Hall, "A Model for Coping with Role Conflict."

23. Ibid.

24. See, for example, Jones and Korchin, eds., *Minority Mental Health*; Anthony Marsella and Paul B. Pedersen, eds., *Cross-Cultural Counseling and Psychotherapy* (New York: Pergamon Press, 1981); and Richard H. Dana, ed., *Human Services for Cultural Minorities* (Baltimore, Md.: University Park Press, 1981).

Income Security:
The Case of Nonwhite Children

Martha N. Ozawa

With the election of Ronald Reagan to the White House in 1980, the old political doctrine of "the government that does the least is the best government" was reincarnated as a political slogan, "get government off the back of the people." Faithful to this slogan, the present Administration moved swiftly to cut social welfare expenditures, primarily for the poor, among whom nonwhite families are overrepresented.[1] Although these cuts were deplorable, they may spur social workers to reevaluate the effectiveness of the current programs that purport to ensure income security for poor children, especially nonwhite poor children.

Concerns for poor children and nonwhite children go hand in hand in this nation because the probability that nonwhite families will be poor is about 2.5 times that of white families.[2] Thus, social policy that sets a floor on income for children is particularly pertinent for nonwhite children. (In this article, "nonwhite children" denotes black, American Indian, Mexican American, and Asian American children, as well as the children of recent immigrants from Asian and African countries.)

In the past, this country provided basic income security for poor children reluctantly, as though they were an extra burden on society. It seemed that if the government had its own way, it would not have ensured these children minimally adequate income security. However, current trends in birth rates and immigration may force

Reprinted from *Social Work*, 28 (September–October 1983), pp. 347–353.

the public and governmental officials to reevaluate national policy and programs on income support for children. Because of higher birth rates among nonwhites than among whites and because of a relatively greater number of nonwhite immigrants coming from Asia and Africa, the trend toward a greater representation of non-whites in the nation's population is accelerating. In 1960, the proportion of nonwhites in the United States was only 11 percent; in 1980, it was 17 percent.[3]

It is imperative that nonwhite children—the growing segment of the population—be allowed to reach their full potential so they will become an important source of national growth, instead of a drain on national resources. Whether this country becomes vigorous and productive again may well depend on how quickly and thoroughly nonwhite children can join the mainstream of society. Furthermore, income maintenance programs must be developed that not only provide an adequate minimum level of income for children but that have the least degree of adverse secondary effects on children and their parents.

This article evaluates the current major income maintenance programs that affect the economic well-being of children—nonwhite children in particular—and suggests an alternative approach to providing income security for children. More specifically, the author explains why social security does not meet the needs of nonwhite children as much as those of white children. In addition, she examines problems associated with welfare programs, giving special attention to Aid to Families with Dependent Children (AFDC), and discusses the economic and noneconomic impacts of such programs. Also, she explores the impact of various types of income maintenance programs on the distribution of white and nonwhite families who are poor and suggests alternative income security programs for children, which she believes would have less adverse side effects.

INCOME MAINTENANCE FOR NONWHITE CHILDREN

Social security (that is, old-age, survivors, and disability insurance) has become a powerful income maintenance program not only for the elderly but also for the children of this nation. In 1982, about 3.7 million children—or 10 percent of the total number of beneficiaries—benefited from the program. Of the estimated $157 billion expended for social security that year, $10 billion—or 6.4 percent—was distributed to child beneficiaries.[4]

Table 1.

Average Monthly Dependent Benefits per Child, by Race and Type of Insurance, 1979[a]

Type of Insurance	All	White	Nonwhite
Old age insurance			
Benefits per worker	$294.30	$299.10	$246.00
Benefits per child	119.20	128.40	92.00
As percentage of the worker's benefit[b]	(41)	(43)	(37)
Disability insurance			
Benefits per worker	322.00	329.70	283.40
Benefits per child	95.20	100.30	78.10
As percentage of the worker's benefit[b]	(30)	(30)	(28)
Survivors insurance			
Average primary insurance amount of deceased workers	307.60	—[c]	—[c]
Benefits per child	201.70	216.20	159.90
As percentage of the worker's benefit[b]	(66)	—[c]	—[c]

SOURCE: *Social Security Bulletin, Annual Statistical Supplement, 1981* (Washington, D.C.: Social Security Administration, 1983), Tables 66 and 107, pp. 123–134, 177–178.

[a] Data include 435,000 disabled children aged 18 and over, and 793,000 students aged 18–21.

[b] Expressed as a percentage of average monthly benefits of workers (primary insurance amount under survivors insurance).

[c] Data not available.

A disproportionately large number of nonwhite children benefited from the program. Although nonwhite children constituted 17 percent of the total population of children, 26 percent of the child beneficiaries were nonwhite.[5] However, if one focuses on benefits per child, a different picture emerges: nonwhite children do not benefit from social security as much as do white children.

Table 1 compares the pattern of the benefits received in 1979 by nonwhite children and white children. Nonwhite children consistently received smaller benefits than did white children, both in absolute amounts and in the percentage of benefits for workers of respective racial backgrounds. The children of disabled workers may be taken as an example. Children of white disabled workers received, on the average, monthly benefits of $100.30, which represented 30 percent of the average benefit for white disabled workers. In contrast, the average monthly benefit for children of nonwhite disabled workers was only $78.10, or 28 percent of the average benefit for such workers.

How can one explain such benefit differentials among children in relation to racial backgrounds? These differentials occur because the level of benefits for child beneficiaries is a function of two factors: (1) the level of earnings of primary beneficiaries (workers) and (2) family size. The first factor is self-explanatory, but the second requires clarification. The benefit structure of social security is designed to prevent the sum of all benefits of family members from becoming too high in relation to the level of workers' earnings before the onset of risks—old age, disability, and death of the breadwinner—recognized under the law. To achieve this objective, the program provides the maximum *family* benefit for a worker's level of average indexed monthly earnings (AIME) (that is, the lifetime average monthly earnings of a worker after adjusting for increases in average wages over time). Thus, even though each child is nominally entitled to a percentage of the primary insurance amount (PIA)—50 percent under old age insurance (OAI) and disability insurance (DI) and 75 percent under survivors insurance (SI)—benefits for dependents in large families are proportionately decreased so that the sum of benefits of workers and dependents in the family comes down to the maximum family benefit.

The impact of earnings levels and family size is clearly reflected in the benefits that nonwhite children receive. Compared to white children, nonwhite children on social security suffer not only from being born to a large family but also from their parents' low levels of earnings. There is another complexity here. The maximum family benefit is generally a smaller multiple of the PIA if earnings are low rather than high.[6] What happens is that a relative advantage given to low earners in calculating PIAs is partially undone when maximum family benefits are calculated. PIAs—basic benefits for workers themselves—are higher for low-wage earners in proportion to their previous earnings (AIME) than for high-wage earners. But maximum family benefits are calculated so the proportionality in the relationship between previous earnings and benefits is restored —not completely, but substantially. Thus, in the final analysis, the factors that hurt nonwhite children are basically family size and their parents' levels of earnings, and the social security program is not well designed to counteract these disadvantageous factors completely.

Of all the social insurance programs, social security is most dedicated to implementing the principle of social adequacy. That is, social security specifies that children and dependent spouses of insured workers receive a fraction of the workers' basic benefit. Yet even the social security program goes just so far in meeting family needs. Large families do not receive proportionately large benefits. Lawmakers' hesitation to provide benefits to an indefinite number of dependents without imposing a maximum stems from their belief that social insurance benefits should be earned—that is, benefits should be tied to the level of previous earnings. Moreover, they believe that benefits so obtained should be no greater than what the worker earned before the onset of risks recognized under the law. In such a philosophical context, it is unlikely that social security could be reformed to accommodate the needs of all children, nonwhite children in particular. A solution must be found outside the context of social security.

AFDC is a major publicly supported income maintenance program that provides cash payments for children in low-income families. In June 1981, 7.6 million children were supported under the program. In addition, in 1981, 400,000 children benefited from AFDC-UP (AFDC for unemployed parents), in operation in twenty-four states and the District of Columbia. Under these two programs, approximately $9 billion in benefits were distributed to support children in 1981.[7]

Children on AFDC have a high probability of being on other welfare programs as well. A study shows that the likelihood that AFDC families will participate in Medicaid is 99 percent; in the Food Stamp program, 60 percent; and in the public housing program, 14 percent.[8] These statistics indicate that a sizable proportion of children and their families are dependent on an interlocking package of welfare programs. Many working and nonworking families with children use one or more of these programs to escape from or ameliorate their poverty.

CONTROVERSY OVER WELFARE PROGRAMS

That the income security of low-income families is dealt with through welfare programs arouses controversy and political passion from time to time. Indeed, some politicians tend to blame these programs, at least in part, for the economic malaise in this country. Why, then, are these programs so controversial?

AFDC and other welfare programs are controversial because they are believed to create adverse secondary effects, even though they achieve the policy objective of providing income support efficiently to a targeted population. Major adverse secondary effects of AFDC and other welfare progams involve the following areas: (1) work incentives and (2) the stigmatization and political coercion of recipients of benefits.

Possible Effect on Work Incentives

All welfare programs now in operation involve some kind of income testing. Economists point out that both the basic guarantee (the amount of the transfer payments to families who have no income of their own) and the benefit withdrawal rate (the rate at which benefits are withdrawn as income rises) are closely tied to the issue of work incentives.

Concern about work incentives is compounded if a family participates in several welfare programs simultaneously. As was already mentioned, many AFDC families receive Medicaid, food stamps, public housing assistance, and perhaps other benefits. In such cases, during the first four months of AFDC recipiency, the AFDC program reduces its payments by sixty-seven cents for each dollar of earnings after the families pay for child care and work expenses and keep thirty dollars to themselves. When families stay on the program for more than four months, the program reduces its payments dollar for dollar against earnings after child care and work expenses are paid. Both the Food Stamp program and the public housing program reduce their benefits by a percentage of earnings. Medicaid is provided as long as the family is on AFDC. Since all the programs except Medicaid reduce benefits simultaneously as earnings increase, in essence, these programs together "tax away" earnings at a cumulative implicit (that is, unstated or unofficial) tax rate of considerable magnitude. Furthermore, the family has to pay social security taxes at 6.7 percent on all earnings and may have to pay income taxes as well. A study by Hausman showed that, under these circumstances, even families who can keep the first thirty dollars and one-third of the remainder of their earnings are confronted with a cumulative implicit tax rate of at least 76 percent.[9] Thus, the cumulative implicit tax rate for families who stay on AFDC for more than four months is expected to be as high as or even higher than 100 percent! Moreover, when recipient families earn more than the cutoff point of AFDC, they are dropped from Medicaid, thus creating the problem of a decline in total family income despite greater earnings.

Indeed, several studies have confirmed policymakers' concerns over the effect of welfare programs on work incentives. Garfinkel and Orr found that the employment rate of female heads of households on AFDC declined as the basic guarantee increased. They also found that the implicit tax rate adversely affected the employment rate.[10] Studies by Williams and Saks and by Hausman reported similar findings.[11]

Both theoretical analyses and empirical studies by economists indicate that many low-income families may be trapped, by their own choice or otherwise, in the system of welfare programs and may find it difficult to earn enough to move out of the system. This is especially the case for nonwhite families, who have a larger number of dependents to support.[12] Because welfare programs calculate assistance payments on the basis of family size, the basic guarantee for a large family is higher than the guarantee for a small family. As a consequence, the break-even point (the level of earnings at which the family gets off welfare) is that much higher. Indeed, Gibbons found that the number of children in a family is a statistically significant predictor of the length of time a family stays on AFDC, when other variables in the study are controlled.[13]

Suppose, for instance, that identical twin sisters, who have the same qualifications and backgrounds for receiving welfare except for number of children, receive AFDC. The basic guarantee will be greater for the familiy with more children; consequently, the cutoff point at which this family can pull itself out of AFDC will be higher. Thus, this family has a greater probability of being trapped in the welfare system than does the family headed by the other twin sister, even though both sisters may be equally motivated to work and may work the same number of hours.

Not knowing the basis for calculating transfer payments, the public might erroneously accuse the twin sister who has a larger number of children of immorality and lack of motivation to work. Her children too might have to suffer from the public's characterization, however mistaken, of their mother. Family size, which is the decisive factor that differentiates the fate of the two hypothetical families headed by twin sisters, is totally beyond the control of the children. One can imagine that many nonwhite children are in a predicament exactly like this one.

Stigmatization and Political Coercion

The stigmatization of recipients of welfare has gone hand in hand with the public's belief in the work ethic. In this work-oriented society, welfare recipients who have the potential for work are stigmatized. Stigmatization acts as a means of social control and as a preventive mechanism in that feelings of degradation tend to prevent many individuals from applying for assistance payments.

Although stigmatization fulfills a function, its effects on those who are already on welfare may be devastating. The tendency of nonrecipients to stereotype welfare recipeints with respect to lifestyle, motivation, and attitudes has been extensively investigated.[14] Because of stigma, the receipt of welfare results in recipients' self-depreciation.[15]

Regulation of Lives

The day-to-day activities of an increasing number of heads of low-income families have come under governmental regulations as a result of the enactment of new welfare programs and the expansion of existing ones during the War on Poverty. In the 1960s and early 1970s, Medicaid was introduced for recipients of public assistance and for the medically indigent, state programs of adult public assistance were transformed into the federal Supplemental Security Income (SSI) program, the Basic Education Opportunity Grants (BEOG) were initiated, the Food Stamp program was nationalized, and a program of earned income tax credits was enacted. There was also an enormous growth in payments under AFDC and an expansion of work and training programs during that period. The proliferation of income-tested welfare programs has meant that a greater number of families are participating not only in individual programs but in more than one program. The families receiving multiple benefits report to several governmental agencies. Furthermore, if they are out of work, they may be questioned about why they are out of work, why they are unwilling to take a job offered by the employment office, and so on. Different agencies might ask similar questions over and over again.

The government's regulation of the lives of recipient families increases as more and more working families are allowed to participate in welfare programs. When families receiving welfare were largely those deemed unemployable—such as the aged, the disabled, and single-headed families with preschool children—the issue of the work incentive was not paramount. But the inclusion of working families has necessitated the incorporation of specific rules and regulations in welfare programs to ensure that the work effort of household heads is maintained. One example is the stipulation that AFDC mothers without preschool children are required to participate in the Work Incentive Program. Another example is the stipulation that unemployed fathers of families receiving food stamps must report to the local employment agency; if they refuse to accept a job offered through the agency, the family will be denied food stamps.

What does all this mean to nonwhite children and especially to children of nonwhite immigrants? Nonwhite children of families that depend heavily on welfare probably see the world differently from the way white, middle-class children do. They probably see that their parents' work does not improve their family's financial well-being commensurate with how hard the parents work. Their family cannot accumulate savings while on welfare. These children may realize that their parents' daily lives are regulated by the government. The world perceived by nonwhite children of poor families on welfare is a far cry from the image that this country projects abroad or to most of its citizens.

Many immigrants, some of them political refugees, come to the United States in search of better economic opportunities. If they get involved in the welfare system, the chances are great that they may become trapped in welfare, with all its undesirable connotations. Unless they succeed in getting off welfare quickly, they may be forced to join the underclass that is dealt with by the government under rules and regulations different from those that apply to the mainstream of the nation. Living under such conditions is not conducive to bringing nonwhite children into the mainstream of society.

IMPACT ON RACIAL COMPOSITION

Although the United States spends an enormous amount of money for income maintenance purposes, income transfer programs are not erasing the color line between the affluent and the poor. Rather, they are intensifying it.

Table 2 shows the percentage distribution of poverty in white and nonwhite families in 1976 at the following cumulative stages of income definition: (1) before any transfer was distributed, (2) after cash payments from social insurance programs were added

Table 2.

Percentage Distribution of Families below the Poverty Level, by Race
under Alternative Income Definitions, 1976

Race	Income before any Transfer	Income after Cash Payments from Social Insurance Programs[a]	Income after Cash Payments from Welfare Programs[b]	Income after In-Kind Benefits from Welfare Programs[c]	Income after Benefits from Medicare and Medicaid
White	80.8	74.7	74.7	74.0	76.8
Nonwhite	19.2	25.3	25.3	26.0	23.2
Total	100.0	100.0	100.0	100.0	100.0

SOURCE: Derived from U.S. Congress, Congressional Budget Office, *Poverty Status of Families under Alternative Definitions of Income* (rev. ed.; Washington, D.C.: U.S. Government Printing Office, 1977), Table 5, p. 11.

[a] Social insurance includes social security and Railroad Retirement, governmental pensions, unemployment insurance, workers' compensation, and veterans' compensation.

[b] Welfare programs for cash payments include veterans' pensions, Supplemental Security Income, and Aid to Families with dependent Children.

[c] Welfare programs for in-kind benefits include food stamps, child nutrition, and housing assistance.

to income, (3) after cash payments from welfare programs were added to income, (4) after in-kind benefits from welfare programs, except Medicare and Medicaid, were added to income, and (5) after benefits (equivalent to average benefits) from Medicare and Medicaid were added to income.

The table shows clearly that all income maintenance programs combined help less to pull nonwhite families than white families out of poverty. Consequently, after the government distributed all types of benefits, nonwhite families in 1976 constituted a larger percentage of the poor than before these benefits were distributed. More specifically, before transfers, nonwhite families made up 19 percent of all pretransfer poor families. But after transfers, they represented 23 percent of all posttransfer families.

Tracing the impact of income maintenance programs on racial distribution through different stages of income definition, one observes the potent effects of social insurance benefits—mainly social security benefits. The distribution of social insurance benefits makes nonwhite families more concentrated among the poor. Cash payments from welfare programs and in-kind benefits, other than Medicare and Medicaid, keep the racial composition of the poor basically intact. Medicare and Medicaid have the reverse relationship, making nonwhite families slightly less concentrated among the poor than before benefits from these programs were distributed to eligible recipients.

Why do income maintenance programs cause a greater concentration of nonwhite families among the poor? Whether a family is brought out of poverty by receiving benefits from an income maintenance program depends not only on the amount of benefits but also on the family's pretransfer income and family size. That is, given a certain amount of benefits, the probability is higher that the family will be brought out of poverty if it has a relatively high pretransfer income than if it has a low pretransfer income. Furthermore, because poverty-line income is a function of family size, small families find it relatively easier to pull themselves out of poverty than do large families.

Since social insurance benefits are tied to previous earnings, benefits for white families tend to be higher. These benefits are used to fill a relatively small poverty gap (the difference between poverty-line income and the income available before transfer payments) because white families tend to have a higher pretransfer income and a smaller family size than do nonwhite families. The relative insensitivity of social insurance programs to meeting the needs of families as a unit (as indicated in Table 1, for instance) further aggravates the situation for nonwhite families.

Income-tested welfare programs—whether for cash payments or in-kind benefits—and Medicare and Medicaid are effective in helping nonwhite families; these programs pull basically similar percentages of white and nonwhite families out of poverty after the impact of social insurance benefits is felt. This is not to say that income-tested welfare programs bring a greater percentage of nonwhite families out of poverty than do social insurance programs. On the contrary, social insurance programs are more potent in helping nonwhite and white families out of poverty than are welfare programs.[16] But still the effects of these welfare programs are not so drastic as to improve the racial composition of the poor.

What are the reasons for the relative impotence of income-tested welfare programs in changing the racial composition of the poor, even though welfare programs presumably have been developed to mitigate the unequal distribution of income from private sources—such as earnings, interest, rent, and dividends—and to make up for the inadequacy of social insurance programs in meeting the needs of low-income families? Again, the answer is found in the relatively low level of pretransfer income of nonwhite families. Because the income of these families from private sources is low and because their benefits from social insurance programs are also relatively low, nonwhite families require that welfare programs fill a relatively large poverty gap, which is further accentuated by the relatively large family size of nonwhites.

In broader philosophical terms, welfare programs in a society dedicated to a free economic system have inherent limitations. In such a society, welfare programs can soften the hardship of poverty but cannot reshape the ranking of families' economic well-being— a ranking that stems from the distribution of earnings and earnings-related social insurance benefits. If welfare programs should go too far in distorting this ranking, the incentive structure in a free economy would be threatened, and political passion against the recipients of welfare payments would intensify.

ALTERNATIVE APPROACHES

Is there a way to provide for nonwhite children adequately without creating adverse secondary effects? To find an answer, one needs to learn from the experience of the current system of income maintenance programs. That is, the current system of income support cannot provide an adequate income to nonwhite children without creating adverse secondary effects, such as a high cumulative implicit tax rate, stigma, and governmental regulations.

As the foregoing discussion indicated, social insurance programs, although popular with the general public, cannot provide adequately for children—and nonwhite children in particular—because benefits are tied to previous earnings. Welfare programs, which attempt to provide benefits on the basis of family size, provide for children only at the risk of creating concern about disincentive effects and imposing stigma and governmental regulations on the children and their parents. Thus, the basic problem inherent in the current way of providing for children is that the government is attempting to establish income security for children through programs that are closely tied to the work status and the earnings levels of their parents. Even if a program is established specifically to provide for children (for example, AFDC), its primary goal changes over time from providing income for children to regulating the lives of recipient families if benefits provided are contingent on the work status and the earnings levels of their parents. In a free economy, the difficulty of establishing income security for children derives from the basic gap between the way the head of the household earns income and the way family need is defined. Earnings are made through individual effort; family need is defined by the number of individuals sharing the same household.

One way to reconcile the concern about providing adequately for children with that of maintaining the work incentives of their parents is to provide income support for children independently of their parents' work status and earnings levels. There are two ways to do this: (1) refundable tax credits for children and (2) children's allowances. Both alternatives take the form of "demogrants" to redistribute income. The term "demogrant" means a universal provision of flat-amount benefits to all individuals who fall within a certain category identified under the law.[17]

Refundable Tax Credits for Children

A program of refundable tax credits allows parents to claim tax credits for their children against their income taxes. Under such a program, if parents are too poor to pay income taxes, the government sends them a check for the amount of the tax credits. In this way, whatever their income level, all families with children receive the same dollar amount of income support for each child.

Compared with the current personal exemptions for children, such tax credits are more progressive in the distribution of benefits. Under the present system of personal exemptions, the amount of taxes saved is directly related to income levels; the higher the income bracket, the greater the tax savings through the claiming of personal exemptions for children. Under a program of tax credits, taxes saved would be the same across income brackets. Furthermore, through this program, all children would be provided with the same amount of income support regardless of whether their parents paid income taxes.

However, there are some drawbacks to the tax-credit approach of providing income security for children. Taxpayers must file an income tax return to claim tax credits. Chances are great that many children of low-income families would not benefit from the program because low-income parents who have never filed an income tax return might have difficulty in doing so. In addition, recent immigrants might have language problems. In short, the tax-credit approach cannot guarantee provision of income support for all children because, under this approach, the burden of proving the age of children and *applying* for credits rests with the parent.

Children's Allowances

If the federal government decided to adopt a program of children's allowances with the objectives of favoring low-income families and being fiscally efficient, it might provide flat-amount children's allowances to all children and require taxpaying parents to include children's allowances in their taxable income.[18] Taxable children's allowances could form a benefit structure that is more progressive than a program of tax credits. Under taxable children's allowances, the lower the income bracket, the higher the net value of children's allowances; under tax credits, the tax saved would be the same across income brackets.

Both children's allowances and tax credits depart philosophically from current income maintenance programs in important ways. These suggested programs would simply deal with the problem of family size, not with the question of parents' earnings capabilities. In short, the problem of the income insecurity of children would be faced head on. In contrast, current income maintenance programs deal with the income insecurity of children only indirectly through dealing with the parents' earnings capabilities. Thus, under either children's allowances or tax credits, a minimum income security for children could be established, and these alternatives could liberate the parents as well. A policy choice that would maintain work incentives would mean less intervention in the wage structure. Parents could earn all they were able to; they could keep all they earned—subject to income taxes, of course, if they earned enough to pay taxes. Furthermore, they would not be regulated the way current welfare recipients are regulated, nor would their work incentives be sapped as they are under current income maintenance programs.

Probably, neither children's allowances nor tax credits would assure as high a benefit level as does AFDC. However, the basic issue facing policymakers is clear. These alternative programs would be able to disentangle the problem of the income insecurity of children born to large families from the problem of the earnings capabilities of their parents.

The adoption of either alternative would not solve the problem of high cumulative tax rates imposed on families who receive benefits from multiple programs. However, the adoption of either one would lighten the burden on each income-tested program and reduce its scope. Policymakers might move even further toward meeting the basic needs of children by adopting programs such as free lunches and free health services for children. These programs would be provided as an integral part of public education. Thus, through adopting such universal programs, policymakers might be able to eliminate numerous income-tested programs. They could then begin to solve the problem of cumulative implicit tax rates, which are placing the current welfare programs under political pressure.

SUMMARY

For this nation's healthy development, nonwhite children, who are increasing in number at a faster rate than are white children, must become contributors to social and economic progress to their fullest potential. Adoption of a program that specifically addresses income security for children would facilitate this progress. Either a program of children's allowances or one of tax credits for children offers a viable alternative that deserves serious attention by policymakers. It is difficult to estimate the distributive impact on nonwhite children that would result from replacing AFDC with children's allowances or tax credits for children and, as a corollary, eliminating benefits for children as dependents under social security and personal exemptions for children under federal income taxes. However, it seems clear that work incentives would be enhanced and the psychological impact would be positive for nonwhite families. Most important, the adoption of either of these alternatives would weaken the relationship between color and the receipt of welfare payments. If parents could earn more as a result of stronger work incentives, the relationship between color and poverty status might also be weakened. If this were to occur, one could at last say that nonwhite children would have a chance of joining the mainstream of American society.

Notes and References

1. See P.L. 97-035, *Omnibus Budget Reconciliation Act of 1981*, Title XXIII, "Public Assistance Programs," 97th Cong., 1st sess. (Washington, D.C.: U.S. Government Printing Office, 1981).

2. U.S. Congress, Congressional Budget Office, *Poverty Status of Families under Alternative Definitions of Income* (Washington, D.C.: U.S. Government Printing Office, 1977), Table 5, p. 11.

3. U.S. Bureau of the Census, *Statistical Abstracts of the United States: 1979* (100th ed.; Washington, D.C.: U.S. Government Printing Office, 1979), Table 39, p. 35; and U.S. Bureau of the Census, *Statistical Abstracts of the United States: 1981* (102d ed.; Washington, D.C.: U.S. Government Printing Office, 1981), Tables 36, 84, and 130, pp. 32, 58, and 87.

4. U.S. Department of Health and Human Services, *Monthly Benefit Statistics*, No. 7, 1982 (Washington, D.C.: Social Security Administration, 1982), Table 1, p. 1.

5. *Social Security Bulletin, Annual Statistical Supplement, 1981* (Washington, D.C.: Social Security Administration, 1983), Table 66, pp. 123–134; U.S. Bureau of the Census, "Characteristics of the Population below Poverty," *Current Population Reports*, Series P-60, No. 124 (Washington, D.C.: U.S. Government Printing Office, 1980), Table 7, pp. 36–37.

6. For old age insurance (OAI) and survivors insurance (SI), the maximum family benefit is 1.5 times the primary insurance amount (PIA) at the lowest level of earnings, moving up to 1.88 as the PIA increases to the upper-middle range, then tapering off to 1.75 at the highest earnings level. Until June 1980, the maximum family benefit under disability insurance (DI) was calculated on the same basis as under OAI and SI. However, as a result of the Social Security Disability Amendments of 1980, the maximum family benefit for DI beneficiaries was lowered. Thus, since July 1980, the maximum family benefit has been equal to the PIA at the lowest range of the average indexed monthly earnings (AIME), and about 1.5 times the PIA at the middle and highest range of AIME. Under the amendments, the maximum family benefit for DI beneficiaries is either 85 percent of AIME or 150 percent of the PIA (whichever is less), but no less than 100 percent of the PIA. See Office of Legislative and Regulatory Policy, Office of Policy, Social Security Administration, "Social Security Disability Amendments of 1980: Legislative History and Summary of Provisions," *Social Security Bulletin*, 44 (April 1981), pp. 14–31; and Social Security Administration, *Social Security Bulletin, Annual Statistical Supplement, 1981*, p. 34.

7. *Social Security Bulletin*, 46 (January 1983), Tables M29, M30, and M31, pp. 59, 61.

8. Vee Burke and Alair A. Townsend, "Public Welfare and Work Incentives: Theory and Practice," Studies in Public Welfare, Paper No. 14, U.S. Congress, Joint Economic Committee, Subcommittee on Fiscal Policy, 93d Cong., 2d sess. (Washington, D.C.: U.S. Government Printing Office, 1974), p. 12.

9. Leonard J. Hausman, "Cumulative Tax Rates in Alternative Income Maintenance Systems," in Irene Lurie, ed., *Integrating Income Maintenance Programs* (New York: Academic Press, 1975), p. 44.

10. Irwin Garfinkel and Larry Orr, "Welfare Policy and the Employment Rate of AFDC Mothers," *National Tax Journal*, 27 (June 1974), pp. 275–286.

11. Robert Williams, *Public Assistance and Work Effort* (Princeton, N.J.: Princeton University Press, 1975); Daniel Saks, *Public Assistance for Mothers in an Urban Labor Market* (Princeton, N.J.: Industrial Relations Section, Princeton University, 1975); and Jerry Hausman, "Labor Supply," in Henry Aaron and Joseph Pechman, eds., *How Taxes Affect Economic Behavior* (Washington, D.C.: The Brookings Institution, 1981).

12. In 1980, the average number of persons per household was 2.75 for whites and 3.06 for nonwhites. See U.S. Bureau of the Census, *Statistical Abstracts of the United States: 1981,* Table 62, p. 43.

13. Jacque E. Gibbons, "Incentives for Dependency: Non-Cash Benefits in the Aid to Families with Dependent Children Program." Unpublished Ph.D. dissertation, Washington University, St. Louis, Mo., 1981.

14. Joe R. Feagin, "America's Welfare Stereotypes," *Social Science Quarterly,* 52 (March 1974), pp. 921–933.

15. Scott Briar, "Welfare from Below: Recipients' View of the Public Welfare System," *California Law Review,* 54 (May 1966), pp. 370–385.

16. See Martha N. Ozawa, *Income Maintenance and Work Incentives: Toward a Synthesis* (New York: Praeger Publishers, 1982), pp. 71–95.

17. For further discussion of "demogrants," see Martha N. Ozawa, "Issues in Welfare Reform," *Social Service Review,* 52 (March 1978), pp. 37–55.

18. For a detailed discussion of children's allowances, see Ozawa, *Income Maintenance and Work Incentives,* pp. 191–229.

Beyond Cultural Awareness: Preparing Child Welfare Workers for Ethnic-Sensitive Practice

*Pamela Day, Joseph S. Gallegos, Linda Wilson,
Chizuko Norton, Arthur Dodson, and Emily Bruce*

Children of color in the United States continue to be disproportionately represented in the child welfare system. Minority children
are more likely to enter the system, experience multiple placements,
and remain in care longer than nonminority children.[1] Although
children of color are overrepresented in the system, the majority
of child welfare workers and supervisors are white, and only 25
percent of state agencies have training programs that prepare staff
members to work with children and families from racial and ethnic
minority backgrounds.[2] The result of these circumstances may be
stereotyped knowledge and preconceptions that impede the delivery
of culturally sensitive services to minority children and families of
the children.

This article describes a workshop in techniques for training child
welfare workers for ethnic-sensitive practice. In the past, such efforts, often called "cultural awareness training," were not sufficiently
consistent to establish clear links to practice. The training workshop, Beyond Cultural Awareness, was held in November 1981 for
child welfare educators and trainers in Alaska, Idaho, Oregon, and
Washington. The workshop was sponsored by the Northwest Regional Child Welfare Training Center, University of Washington School
of Social Work. The authors conducted the workshop and a six-
month follow-up with participants following the workshop. Because

training in cross-cultural effectiveness is a long-term process, the workshop was designed to assist trainers and educators to prepare child and family service workers for practice with ethnically and culturally diverse groups of clients. The goals were (1) to affirm for participants the importance of cross-cultural training for child and family service workers, (2) to equip them with models for teaching and training ethnic-sensitive practice, and (3) to provide participants with a procedure for applying one or more ethnic-sensitive training approaches in their agency or school and thus to influence child welfare work environments.

An important feature of the workshop was the goal of moving participants beyond the cognitive understanding of cultural differences to the building of skills for cross-cultural helping. To this end, the focus was on generic principles of practice that transcend specific ethnic groups and which provide a theoretical base for ethnic-sensitive practice. To bridge the gap between theory and practice, an individual planning process was incorporated through which participants were taught to apply what they had learned to practice. Furthermore, to assure the implementation of the behavior-change plans, each participant was followed up and his or her individual plans were supported by consultation, information on resources, and evaluation. The training was organized in two parts—a two-day training workshop formed the first part and a six-month follow-up formed the second part.

TRAINING WORKSHOP

The training workshop included three major components, entitled Ethnicity and Culture, Ethnic Competence, and Translating Teaching and Training Models to Practice. Individual Plan Building was an important part of the third component and was the focal point for the follow-up.

Ethnicity and Culture

The first component was designed to help participants focus on the importance of ethnicity and culture in their lives and in the lives of the children and families they serve. An ethnicity exercise was utilized to help participants reflect on their ethnicity and to share those observations with others.[3] Participants were divided into small groups of six to eight people to ensure a mixture of professions, cultures, and areas of residence. Each participant answered the following five questions and then, led by a facilitator, discussed each question with the group.

1. What is your ethnic identity?
2. In what locality or community did you grow up, and what other ethnic groups resided in the community?
3. How did your family see itself as like or different from families of other ethnic groups?
4. What are your earliest images of color as an ethnic factor?
5. What are your feelings about your ethnic identity? How might they be influenced by the power relationship between your ethnic group and others?

Participants are encouraged to react to the exercise both personally and as trainers and educators and to discuss its use in the classroom. As underscored by participant evaluations, the exercise was a powerful tool that encouraged introspection and interaction and enabled participants to examine and discuss their attitudes and feelings toward their ethnic identities and to hear the personal experiences of others. Coming at the beginning of the workshop, it provided a framework for cultural awareness as well as a model of involvement by participants.

Ethnic Competence

The second component focused on the ethnic competence model—a generic model for cross-cultural teaching and training. The didactic presentation of theory was enhanced by the use of a videotape, "Minority Views," and a small-group exercise in which participants applied the ethnic competence framework to case material.[4]

The ethnic competence model describes a structured approach to the assessment by social workers of their awareness, sensitivity, and skill in providing services to clients who are culturally different from them. It also suggests a framework for competence in cross-cultural practice and is a teaching tool. As a teaching device, the model guides instructors in developing curricula. Instructors utilize the same principles they will be teaching their trainees and view curriculum development as a standard problem-solving process of assessing needs, identifying problems, and devising an appropriate course of action. The model and its key elements—assessment, the help-seeking-behavior model, and empowerment—are described fully in "The Ethnic Competence Model for Social Work

Education" by Joseph S. Gallegos, which appears elsewhere in this volume (see pp. 1–9).

It should be noted that although the model was presented as a generic framework for cross-cultural training, the material, as presented, has certain limitations. First, cultural awareness and cultural awareness training are two separate entities. Second, there are two levels of cultural awareness—awareness of cultural differences (a phase in which knowledge is accumulated and integrated) and translating awareness into action (an analytic and evaluative function). Although the ethnic competence model implies action, as a foundation curriculum, it does not provide specialized content. Rather, an underlying assumption of the model is that trainers will develop supplementary training materials that are specific to their needs.[5]

Translating the Model into Practice

To integrate theory and practice, three techniques were used in the training workshop. The first technique was small-group discussions of issues of assessment in relation to specific minority groups. The second technique involved consultation with minority resource persons both individually and in groups. The third technique was to have each participant develop his or her ethnic competence in a specific work setting.

Assessment in small groups. After the presentation of material, participants were divided into small groups to discuss the ethnic group in which they were most interested. Each group was asked to utilize the following framework for discussing a specific case:

1. What is the client's perception of his or her problem? Look for cultural elements, such as belief systems, customs, networks, community involvement, self-concept, and the role of significant others.

2. What is the worker's perception? How is this perception defined and according to whom? To what extent is the perception determined by the worker's belief system and by the function or capacity of the agency?

3. What is the motivation for change? How is it determined by the worker and the client? What elements of strength and hope are to be found in the situation, and what outside supports and barriers can be determined?

4. What resistance to change can be identified? Are the barriers realistic? Are these barriers internalized cultural boundaries? Are

they external to the minority community or are they attributable to the dominant cultural suprasystem?

5. To what degree is the client's concept of his or her self-worth involved in the client's difficulty in overcoming the problem? To what degree has the process of acculturation and assimilation enhanced or exacerbated the client's ability to cope with the stress of sociocultural dissonance?

Group members also were given the following goals for ethnically sensitive practice:

1. To help the client achieve mastery and competence.

2. To help the client establish and utilize a support network.

3. To help the client identify and use positive opportunities for performance.

4. To help the client exercise self-determination.

Resource persons. The second technique further structured the participants' incorporation of the material. In addition, it helped participants to begin thinking about building their own plans and to become more experienced in the valuable processes of networking and the utilization of resources. The resource portion of the workshop included a resource fair, designed to acquaint participants with a variety of models for cross-cultural teaching and training and to provide them with concrete assistance with their teaching and training plans. Resource persons from a variety of cultural training projects met in small groups with participants, sharing their teaching or training efforts and leading discussions. After the group discussions, they met individually with interested participants to provide consultation on individual training plans.

A panel discussion on barriers to cross-cultural teaching and training and strategies for overcoming them brought together five persons with expertise in that area. Panelists gave examples from their own experience to illustrate their answers to the following questions:

1. Describe some of the major barriers you have encountered in planning and conducting cultural awareness training.

2. What are some of the means you used to overcome these barriers? Which techniques were most successful?

3. Do you have any suggestions about the marketing or packaging of training plans and how to marshall support for the plan in your agency or school?

4. What have you found to be most effective in gaining administrative support for training plans?

5. The lack of resources is often a major barrier to cultural awareness training. Describe some of your efforts to develop resources

and offer some guidelines for the development of effective resources.

Developing individual plans. This section of the workshop involved participants in developing cross-cultural training or teaching plans. Two exercises were conducted. For each exercise, participants worked together in small groups with a resource person who acted as a consultant. Planning guidelines, sample planning sheets, and worksheets were provided. In the first exercise, participants were asked to develop three major goals of ethnic-sensitive practice that they would like to achieve in their agency or school. For each goal, they identified the corresponding need or problem, the expected impact of the achievement of the goal, and the rationale for selecting the goal. During the second exercise, which took place after the resource portion of the workshop, participants chose one goal to be developed and formalized into a specific training plan and identified objectives that might be reached within three months. These objectives specified resources, strategies for implementing the goal, and barriers to achieving it. In addition, they could set some long-range objectives to be reached in one, two, or three years.

The following questions were used to review each participant's plan:

1. Is the plan feasible?
2. What is the rationale for the overall goal of the plan?
3. What suggestions would you make to improve the plan?

At the conclusion of the workshop, some participants presented their plans to the group. These plans represented a mix of settings (both schools and agencies) and provided the basis for discussion, critiques, and suggestions of strategies and resources. Then all the participants submitted their plans to training staff, who described the follow-up process.

FOLLOW-UP

The follow-up was conducted for six months. It included the evaluation of participants' individual work plans; the provision of resource materials requested by participants; in-person, telephone, or written consultation with individual participants regarding implementation of their plans; and feedback from participants about the process.

The follow-up was conducted by a multiethnic committee comprising the people who conducted or who served as resource persons for the workshop. The committee had expertise in cross-cultural training and knew minority resources in the region.

The follow-up committee reviewed each work plan shortly after the workshop. It then wrote to each group member, suggesting how the work plan could best be implemented and offering additional resources. Participants were sent either resource materials or information about publications and the procedures for and cost of obtaining relevant material. When possible, committee members met individually with participants to provide assistance and consultation. (Additional follow-up activities could include the provision of specific resource packages, such as an annotated bibliography for faculty that focuses on the integration of cross-cultural content in the social work curriculum.)

In the final portion of the follow-up, participants were asked to assess their experiences in attempting to implement their work plans. They received a one-page assessment tool and a follow-up telephone call.

Evaluation

In general, the participants rated the workshop as valuable. A majority of the participants (71 percent) found that the learning objectives were adequately and more than adequately met; and 76 percent thought that the program activities had assisted them in meeting the learning objectives. The most useful aspects of the program, according to the participants, included the ethnic-identity exercises, the presentation on translating training concepts into practice, and consultation with resource persons. Negative comments concerned the need for more details about translating the model into practice and the unmet expectation of learning specific content rather than a conceptual model.

The participants judged follow-up to be helpful, although they reported varying success in implementing their work plans. The overall evaluation suggests that the process of attending the workshop, developing a training plan, and attempting to implement a work plan reaffirmed for the participants the importance of cross-cultural training for child and family service workers and provided them with increased knowledge of cross-cultural teaching and training models. Translating these attitudes and this knowledge into practice proved difficult, however. Participants cited such barriers as the lack of money, time, and administrative commitment. Nevertheless, they considered the model useful, and several participants reported making gains in the cross-cultural training efforts in which they were engaging.

CONCLUSION

The ethnic competence model has great promise for training and practice, and its utility will increase when the behavioral components of ethnically competent practice are identified. Work toward this end is under way by the authors. The rationale for this work is that if social services are to be extended equally to all, appropriate competencies for practice must be established. Therefore, the authors make the following recommendations:

1. Agencies and programs must be committed to the implementation of cross-cultural training and practice. The commitment must include time, staff, and money.

2. Cross-cultural training cannot occur without an opportunity to interact with ethnic minority individuals, such as resource persons or agencies. Further, the interaction should not be on a crisis-only basis but should be on ongoing reciprocal relationship.

3. Cross-cultural training requires extensive follow-up and is a lengthy process.

4. For practitioners, the translation of the attitudes, skills, and knowledge of ethnic competence must be reflected in practice.

The training workshop reported in this article was designed to have an impact on the child welfare system by training trainers in ethnic sensitivity. A cultural awareness framework was presented to participants. But, unlike the usual workshop approach in which a one-shot exposure is not enough, a planning technique was utilized to structure the ongoing incorporation of content. This added technique was vital to the success of the workshop in moving participants beyond cultural awareness to setting and attempting to achieve their own objectives and goals. For example, some participants who were social work educators incorporated minority content into their courses, a trainer in Alaska developed a minority resource network, and a child welfare worker developed and shared resource materials on minority groups. Outcomes such as these, the authors think, are empowering in the full sense of ethnic competence.

Notes and References

1. David Fanshel and Eugene B. Shinn, *Children in Foster Care: A Longitudinal Investigation* (New York: Columbia University Press, 1978).

2. *National Survey: In-Service Training for Child Welfare* (Ann Arbor: National Child Welfare Training Center, University of Michigan School of Social Work, 1982).

3. This exercise was adapted from Elaine Pinderhughes, "Teaching Empathy

in Cross-Cultural Social Work," *Social Work*, 24 (July 1979), pp. 312–316; and James W. Green, *Cultural Awareness in the Human Services* (Englewood Cliffs, N.J.: Prentice Hall, 1982), p. 214.

4. Satsuki Tomine, *Minority Views*, video tape, 25 minutes, color (Corvallis, Oreg.: Department of Family Life, Oregon State University, 1978).

5. In the field of child welfare, a number of specialized training programs have been developed to meet the needs of minority groups. See, for example, *Providing Child Welfare Services in a Multi-Cultural Society* (Washington, D.C.: Creative Associates, 1981); Frank F. Montalvo et al., *Mexican American Culture Simulator for Child Welfare: Case Work Vignettes* (San Antonio, Tex.: Our Lady of the Lake University of San Antonio, 1981); Jualynne E. Dodson, *An Afro-Centric Training Manual: Toward a Non-Deficit Perspective in Services to Children and Families* (Knoxville: University of Tennessee School of Social Work, 1982); and J. Wong and J. Banerian, eds., *ICHE Cultural Awareness Training Manual* (San Diego, Calif.: Indochinese Community Health & Education Project, 1980).

Being Responsive to the Chicano Community: A Model for Service Delivery

Rodolfo Arroyo and Sandra A. López

In the last fourteen years, there has been a significant increase in the number of Hispanic people in this country. There has been an even more notable increase in the Hispanic population of Houston, Texas, and its surrounding Harris County—the area discussed in this article. From 1970 to 1980, the Hispanic population increased 61 percent in the United States as a whole, 87.9 percent in Houston, and 98.7 percent in Harris County—the largest county in Texas. As of 1980, Hispanics represented 17.6 percent of the population of the city of Houston, and 15.3 percent of Harris County.[1]

However, the number of linguistically and culturally appropriate counseling services for Spanish-speaking people has not increased proportionately. The limited number of such services prompted the Family Service Center of Houston and Harris County to establish El Centro Familiar (ECF)—an office to serve the Hispanic community, especially Chicanos—the largest group of Hispanics in Houston. ECF is one of several district offices of the Family Service Center. It was established to serve the Chicano population, particularly the residents of the Magnolia *barrio*. It is located in a census tract that has the highest density of Chicanos in Houston.

The services delivered by ECF are the same as those provided by the other district offices of the Family Service Center: counseling and therapy to individuals, couples, families, and groups. However, the ECF staff members also conduct family life education programs. The counseling and therapeutic services at ECF are offered to clients in both English and Spanish.

The authors' experience as social workers at ECF led them to recognize the need for flexibility in and the modification of existing programmatic approaches for serving Chicanos. The development and implementation of these unique approaches directed the authors to conceptualize a model for delivering services to the Chicano community. The model is unique in that it is applicable to a family service setting and it is responsive to the Chicano community. A review of the literature clearly supports the uniqueness of this model.

REVIEW OF THE LITERATURE

The recent literature concerning Chicanos and other Spanish-speaking people has concentrated on such areas as treatment and the delivery of services, cultural considerations, and the utilization of community mental health services. One such article concluded that Chicanos are underrepresented among the clientele of mental health services and that the quality of mental health care provided to them is lower than that of services to any other identifiable population.[2] Acosta carefully examined a number of barriers affecting the use of mental health services by Chicanos, such as the relationship between social class and the treatment offered, stereotypes of folk psychiatry, limitations imposed by language differences, and the effects of stereotypes that Anglo Americans and Chicanos hold about each other.[3]

Barrera stated that rather than focusing solely on the attitudes and perceptions of clients, research needs to be done on evaluating the responsiveness and effectiveness of services. As he put it:

> Given a social context of unresponsive services and a notable absence of bilingual-bicultural professionals, factors such as negative attitudes towards mental health care and the subsequent utilization of non-mental health professionals, i.e., family physicians, can conceivably be perceived as *results* of inadequate service rather than *causes* of underutilization.[4]

In their study of a family service office serving the Chicano community of Fort Worth, Texas, Watkins and Gonzales found that Chicanos were underrepresented among the agency's clientele by 50 percent.[5] They linked the underutilization of social services by minority groups with the ineffectiveness or irrelevance of traditional methods of service delivery to these groups. However, they also were convinced that traditional social work practice can greatly benefit minorities, particularly if the services are initially provided through outreach. Cameron and Talavera reported that community resources were underutilized by Spanish-speaking people in San Mateo, California, because of language barriers, isolation of the ethnic group, lack of awareness of resources, basic pride in self-sufficiency, and reluctance to become involved with the official bureaucracy.[6]

Most of the articles in the literature have dealt with the utilization by Chicanos of services in community mental health centers. Only three articles published in *Social Work* and *Social Casework* during the past twelve years have referred to the use of family agency services.[7]

SERVICE DELIVERY MODEL

The model developed by the authors has five major components that affect the delivery of services to the Chicano community: location of the agency, visibility of the agency, community awareness, language and cultural uniqueness, and treatment issues.

Location

A prime consideration in providing counseling services to the Chicano community is the geographic location of the agency. Location has often been identified as a causal factor in the underutilization of services by Spanish-speaking people. Locating services in the *barrio* can be advantageous to a family service agency because of the high concentration of Chicanos; it is beneficial to the community because the services are physically accessible to the people who are to be served. It also indicates that the agency is sensitive to the importance of the *barrio* to Chicanos and the Chicano culture.

The *barrio* is an important aspect of Chicano life. It engenders a sense of security in that it serves as a symbol of protection from the unfamiliar culture outside its boundaries and of feelings of belonging and cohesion.[8] In addition, the *barrio* functions as a support system and a social institution.[9] Furthermore, it contains the *panaderias* (Mexican bakeries) and other food shops, *peluquerias* (barbershops), restaurants, bars, movie theaters, and Mexican food-product factories that are essential to the lifestyles of members of the Chicano community.

Visibility of the Agency

An agency becomes visible when it informs the community of the existence and availability of its services. Promoting and advertising services through the media and through community education are the responsibilities of any social service or community agency. Many family service agencies promote their services through "agency interpretations"—the delineation and explanation of services—and the presentation of special topics. These agency interpretations and presentations can be made to staff members in schools, hospitals, community mental health centers, city health clinics, various types of crisis programs, juvenile probation agencies, and churches.

The promotion and advertising of services is essential in the Chicano community because ignorance of available resources is a serious impediment to the use of community resources by the Spanish speaking.[10] In addition to agency interpretations and special topic presentations to other agencies, a family service center in the *barrio* should contact other agencies serving the Chicano community. Although the duplication of services may be an initial concern, it can be alleviated through the coordination of efforts by the various agencies involved.

Publicizing mental health services through the media is a natural approach to reaching the Chicano community and thus to achieving visibility. For example, bilingual and Spanish radio and television programs are becoming more popular. These shows often interview guests who inform Chicano listeners of agency services or discuss problems affecting the Chicano community, such as the abuse of inhalants or cultural issues. The appearance of agency staff members on such shows to discuss services is thus another means of making the agency visible.

Community Awareness

Community awareness is achieved through the continuous updating by an agency of information on the current changes in and the problems and issues affecting the community. Not only does it assure that the agency's programs reflect the needs of the community, but it serves as a mechanism for the communication of relevant issues and the promotion of agency visibility.[11] One way of maintaining community awareness is to develop and maintain linkages with other agencies serving Chicanos. These connections ensure that the agencies will have knowledge of the evolving lifestyles and patterns of immigration-migration and of mobility through a mutual sharing of information.

Participation on boards, committees, task forces, and organizations also promotes community awareness.[12] If the staff of a family service agency has succeeded in promoting the agency's visibility, organizing bodies and planning committees will seek their membership to study the community's needs and to recommend solutions to prevalent problems. Involvement of staff in celebrations in the Chicano community, such as *Fiestas Patrias* or *Cinco de Mayo*, is also a means of being aware of community activities.

Language and Cultural Uniqueness

Many Chicanos, especially new immigrants and the elderly, speak only Spanish, while others, including the well educated, young people, and the middle class, speak only English.[13] However, most Chicanos are bilingual to some extent. According to Marcos and Alpert, bilingualism is "the acquisition and maintenance of two separate language codes—each with its own lexical, syntactic, phonetic and ideational components—and the ability to display proficiency in each language with minimal interference in speech production in either."[14] More commonly, bilingualism is defined as the use of two languages with varying degrees of understanding and proficiency.[15] The prevalent form of bilingualism in the *barrio* is the Chicano language—a dialect that is a fusion of English and Spanish. It includes the mixing of both languages in the same sentence, the "Hispanicization" of certain English words, and the use of terms, phrases, and expressions that reflect the life experiences of Chicanos in the United States.

The Chicano dialect is often criticized by linguistic purists because it does not fit their definition of correct or standard language usage. However, as Steiner noted, this dialect has been evolving over the last four centuries; it has flowered in the *barrios* because it is "entirely adequate and appropriate to time, place, and to circumstance."[16] Chicanos speak this dialect not only because they can express themselves freely in it, but because it reinforces their identity as a group, their ethnic pride, and their shared heritage. Because many Chicanos have had little or no formal education in either language, their mode of expression may be devoid of standard or formal speech; but it is full of the unique, colorful, and creative expressions or idioms they have learned in their families and in the *barrio*.

Many Chicanos, even though they may be bilingual, not only prefer to speak Spanish but also pretend not to speak English. In this way, they avoid dealing with Anglo Americans and other non-Hispanics whom they perceive as being (or who actually are) hostile, insensitive, and prejudiced. Sotomayor suggested that the use of Spanish in this way protects Chicanos from "outside threatening forces."[17] The significance of the Spanish language cannot be over-emphasized, for Spanish has been instrumental in maintaining personal, meaningful relationships that have provided emotional stability for many Chicanos.[18] Even Chicanos who are bilingual often revert to Spanish because it is their first language—their mother tongue—and it has great emotional significance for them. Moreover, Chicanos frequently think in Spanish even when they speak English. It is important to remember this phenomenon, particularly when providing counseling services to Chicanos, because when people experience stress, they tend to regress and use their primary language to express fully their worries, anxieties, fears, and concerns.[19] Furthermore, it must be kept in mind that language reflects an individual's philosophy of life, value system, and (most important) aspects of the personality that one may find difficult to understand or even may not notice without knowledge of the language.

Bilingualism is closely intertwined with biculturalism, since the former is often accompanied by the latter, "which refers to socio-cultural elements that go beyond language."[20] Most Chicanos, even those who are not bilingual, are bicultural. They are the products of the Spanish-Indian *(mestizo)* and Anglo-American cultures. This fusion of cultures has produced the distinct Chicano culture, with its own attributes and behaviors. Biculturalism can be illustrated by conceptualizing it on a continuum. At one end of the continuum are those Chicanos who are "Mexican"; at the other end are those who are Americanized but who have "nonetheless retained vestiges of their Mexican culture, which occasionally surface to regenerate thier pride in their background."[21] Most Chicanos, however, live, to some extent, in two cultural systems (American and Mexican) and have two sets of social behavior.[22]

The phenomenon of biculturalism does not connote a schizo-phrenic existence, although one cannot deny that some Chicanos have difficulty adapting to a bicultural lifestyle. Chestang postulated that to function effectively, individuals who live in two cultures develop a dual response.[23] Indeed, this is the case for many Chicanos. Sotomayor noted that Chicanos who have achieved some flexibility in accommodating and integrating the two sets of cultural stimuli know how to select "appropriate and functional behaviors that provide congruence to [them]."[24] In summary, the authors postulate that *duality of response* and *congruence*, within the context of a *continuum*, are the key concepts to understanding the bicultural experience of Chicanos.

Treatment Issues

A number of treatment issues are integral components of the therapeutic process. The authors have selected those that are especially relevant to counseling Chicanos.

Outreach. Outreach is an essential programmatic approach to reaching the Chicano community. As Watkins and Gonzales noted, outreach efforts can symbolically dramatize an agency's desire to meet the community's needs.[25] Social workers in a family service agency in the *barrio* can incorporate outreach into their services in several ways. For example, although home visits are viewed by some agencies as being unproductive and an inappropriate use of a worker's time, such visits can be a means of intervention with Chicanos when in-office sessions are not possible. Group sessions also may have to be scheduled outside the agency. They may be established in a school with the assistance of the principal, counselors, and teachers. These school contacts allow the development of parent education groups for parents of schoolchildren.

Chicano client/Chicano worker. Munoz discussed the importance of recognizing the difficulties encountered in the relationship between a Chicano client and a Chicano social worker. Because the Chicano social worker has a higher income, education level, and social status than the Chicano client, he or she may feel guilty for having succeeded. Because guilt can be a major factor in the relationship, awareness of such feelings can help the worker identify potential pitfalls in the therapeutic relationship. For example, the worker may overidentify the poor socioeconomic conditions of Chicanos as the contributing factor to their mental health. Although environmental factors can affect an individual's mental health, continually identifying them as the major problem can lead to denying the existence of pathology. Denial of pathology also occurs when the worker considers symptoms only within the context of cultural factors.[26] Cultural perspective is important, but it should not be used to excess. Some Chicano social workers may have the need to rescue their Chicano clients, thus perceiving themselves as messiahs. This can have a negative impact on effectiveness.

Prejudice and discrimination. LeVine and Padilla discussed the importance of skin color to Hispanics.[27] Dark-skinned Chicanos may experience prejudice and discrimination, which leads them to feel inferior and alienated. A Chicano's response to such discrimination can be a denial of ethnicity and an attempt to be more "American" or a struggle to maintain all aspects of the "Mexican" culture. Some Chicanos may be categorized as marginal if they are unable to function in either culture. Many Chicanos, however, are able to achieve a bilingual-bicultural existence.

Language. In their study of language independence, Marcos and Alpert discussed three components of language that affect the process and content of psychotherapy: unavailability, splitting, and language-switching.[28] These three components will be described next.

Unavailability signifies the presence of content in the bilingual client's intrapsychic arena that remains hidden and unexplored because it is independent of the language in which the therapy is conducted. Because this content is beyond the therapist's reach, it cannot be part of the working material. If a bilingual or predominantly Spanish-speaking Chicano enters therapy with an English-speaking therapist, the client may profit only minimally because he or she will not be able to verbalize material that could perhaps be more easily revealed in Spanish. Even though a client may choose to speak English with a bilingual social worker, the worker would be able to encourage the client to speak Spanish, if the client so desired, to work through some of the conflicts that are perhaps more amenable to resolution if they are talked about in Spanish.

Splitting—"deflection of the emotional component of a verbalized idea or experience"—is closely related to unavailability.[29] Splitting occurs when a client speaks in the langauge that is less anxiety provoking. Consequently, the client will verbalize emotionally charged content, but the expected or congruent affect will be absent. The result may be a misconception or an incorrect diagnosis.

Language switching refers to the process of changing from one language to another. Chicanos often switch from English to Spanish and vice versa. This linguistic phenomenon often occurs rapidly and unconsciously, although it may occur on a conscious level as well. Although language switching may facilitate communication for the bilingual client, it mainly offers the client opportunities for resistance that are denied to the monolingual individual. For example, if reporting experiences in the language in which they occurred makes them more real, the client may choose to speak in the more abstract, detached language to avoid anxiety.

Marcos and Alpert's linguistic concepts were formulated in their work with "proficient bilinguals" rather than with "subordinate bilinguals."[30] However, the authors feel that these concepts can be used to some extent in working with Chicanos because many Chicanos are bilingual, but their first language is Spanish (which means that many childhood memories, fantasies, and experiences are associated with their mother tongue), Chicanos often engage in language switching, and some Chicanos are considered to be proficient bilinguals.

CONCLUSION

Although the components of the service delivery model are analytically different, they are interrelated. The hypothesis is that the task of making an agency's services visible to the community is made easier if an agency is located in the *barrio*. At the same time, staff at such an agency will be able to maintain a higher degree of community awareness. This awareness will, in turn, lead to a heightened sensitivity of the language and cultural uniqueness of the Chicano people. An increased understanding of the bilingual-bicultural phenomenon will promote an expanded awareness of treatment issues that need to be considered when working with Chicanos.

A thorough understanding and integration of the concepts described in this article are necessary before the model can be effectively utilized. It is hoped that this framework for service delivery will benefit social workers who are committed to providing sensitive counseling and therapy to Chicanos.

Notes and References

1. U.S. Bureau of the Census, *1980 Census of Population and Housing—Texas* (Series PHC 80-V-45), pp. 4–5, and U.S. Bureau of the Census, *1980 Census of Population and Housing—United States Summary* (Series PHC 80-V-1), p. 4 (Washington, D.C.: U.S. Government Printing Office, March 1981 and April 1981, respectively).

2. Amado M. Padilla, Rene A. Ruiz, and Rodolfo Alvarez, "Community Mental Health Services for the Spanish-Speaking/Surnamed Population," *American Psychologist*, 30 (September 1975), pp. 892–905.

3. Frank Acosta, "Barriers Between Mental Health Services and Mexican Americans: An Examination of a Paradox," *American Journal of Community Psychology*, 7 (1979), pp. 503–520.

4. Manuel Barrera, Jr., "Mexican American Mental Health Service Utilization: A Critical Examination of Some Proposed Variables," *Community Mental Health Journal*, 14 (Spring 1978), p. 44.

5. Ted R. Watkins and Richard Gonzales, "Outreach to Mexican Americans," *Social Work*, 27 (January 1982), pp. 68–73.

6. J. Donald Cameron and Esther Talavera, "An Advocacy Program for Spanish-Speaking People," *Social Casework*, 57 (July 1976), p. 427.

7. Ibid., pp. 427–431; Faustina Ramirez-Knoll, "Casework Services for Mexican-Americans," *Social Casework*, 52 (May 1971), pp. 279–284; and Watkins and Gonzalez, "Outreach to Mexican Americans."

8. Marta Sotomayor, "Mexican American Interaction with Social Systems," in Margaret Mangold, ed., *La Causa Chicana: The Movement for Justice* (New York: Family Service Association of America, 1971), pp. 148–160.

9. Guadalupe Gibson, "Mexican American Children and Their Families," p. 27. Paper presented at the Sixth NASW Professional Symposium, "Social Work Practice: Directions for the 1980's," San Antonio, Texas, November 14–17, 1979.

10. Cameron and Talavera, "An Advocacy Program for Spanish-Speaking People," p. 428.

11. John F. Scott and Melvin Delgado, "Planning Mental Health Programs for Hispanic Communities," *Social Casework*, 60 (October 1979), pp. 451–456.

12. Cameron and Talavera, "An Advocacy Program for Spanish-Speaking People," p. 429.

13. Guadalupe Gibson, "An Approach to Identification and Prevention of Developmental Difficulties Among Mexican-American Children," *American Journal of Orthopsychiatry*, 48 (January 1978), p. 102.

14. Luis R. Marcos and Murray Alpert, "Strategies and Risks in Psychotherapy with Bilingual Patients: The Phenomenon of Language Independence," *American Journal of Psychiatry*, 133 (November 1976), p. 1275.

15. Gibson, "An Approach to Identification and Prevention of Developmental Difficulties Among Mexican-American Children."

16. Stan Steiner, *La Raza: The Mexican Americans* (New York: Harper & Row, 1970), p. 233.

17. Marta Sotomayor, "Mexican-American Interaction with Social Systems," *Social Casework*, 52 (May 1971), p. 322.

18. Ibid., pp. 316–322.

19. Gibson, "An Approach to Identification and Prevention of Developmental Difficulties Among Mexican-American Children."

20. Guadalupe Gibson, Ernesto Gomez, and Yolanda Santos, "Bilingual-Bicultural Service for the Barrio," *Social Welfare Forum, 1973* (New York: Columbia University Press, 1974), p. 219.

21. Gibson, "An Approach to Identification and Prevention of Developmental Difficulties Among Mexican-American Children," p. 103.

22. Gibson, Gomez, and Santos, "Bilingual-Bicultural Service for the Barrio," p. 228.

23. Leon Chestang, "Environmental Influences on Social Functioning: The Black Experience," in Pastora San Juan Cafferty and Leon Chestang, eds., *The Diverse Society: Implications for Social Policy*, (Washington, D.C.: National Association of Social Workers, 1976).

24. Marta Sotomayor, "Language, Culture, and Ethnicity in Developing Self-Concept," *Social Casework*, 58 (April 1977), pp. 201–202.

25. Watkins and Gonzales, "Outreach to Mexican Americans."

26. John A. Munoz, "Difficulties of a Hispanic American Psychotherapist in the Treatment of Hispanic American Patients," *American Journal of Orthopsychiatry*, 51 (October 1981), pp. 646–653.

27. Elaine S. LeVine and Amado M. Padilla, *Crossing Cultures in Therapy: Pluralistic Counseling for the Hispanic* (Monterey, Calif.: Brooks/Cole Publishing Co., 1980).

28. Marcos and Alpert, "Strategies and Risks in Psychotherapy with Bilingual Patients," pp. 1275–1278.

29. Ibid., p. 1277.

30. Ibid., pp. 1275–1278.

Social Work Practice with
Undocumented Mexican Aliens

Ramón M. Salcido

Meeting the needs of groups that are isolated by class and color has been a continuing challenge to the social work profession. By and large, this challenge has not been met in the case of undocumented Mexican aliens—a minority of color, who reside in the Mexican-American *barrio*, and are considered a subgroup of the Mexican-American population. In addition, the social work literature has provided little information on the special service needs of this exploited minority.

"Undocumented aliens" are persons who enter the United States without the necessary legal documents and hence are subject to deportation.[1] The exact number of undocumented Mexican aliens in this country is unknown. The most widely publicized estimate provided to the Immigration and Naturalization Service several years ago by Lesko Associates was 5.2 million.[2] Other studies have estimated that the number may be as high as 12 million.[3] Because of the underground lifestyle of this population, accurate measures cannot be used.

Just as undocumented aliens do not receive the services that the rest of the population takes for granted, they are outside the purview of social work regarding the practice methods that are needed for this group. Although many social workers are aware of Mexican aliens, few social work scholars have written on practice strategies for undocumented aliens. This article reviews the literature on undocumented Mexican aliens, discusses a framework for working with them, and outlines intervention strategies that social workers can use to assist them.

THE LITERATURE

Research

Historically, the research literature on undocumented aliens has attempted to isolate social variables that contributed to the movement of people from Mexico to the United States. Such studies have focused on Mexico's high fertility rate, its economic problems, and the dislocation of its rural population into the labor market of the United States.[4] Dagadag's study to determine the place of origin from which undocumented aliens migrate showed that most of them migrated from central Mexico. It also found that most undocumented aliens were low-skilled laborers who were searching for employment.[5] Frisbe analyzed arrests by the border patrol from 1946 to 1965 and observed that the undocumented aliens had come, not because they were attracted to the United States, but because they were pushed by economic forces in Mexico.[6]

Another type of research consists of personal interviews conducted by interested scholars with unapprehended and apprehended male undocumented Mexican aliens. For example, in 1971, Samora collected data from 493 such men in detention centers and in the community.[7] He concluded that the movement of undocumented aliens contributed to the creation of social problems in the United States. In 1977, the author interviewed undocumented and documented alien families living in an urban *barrio*. His study concluded that these families were experiencing severe psychological stress, were living below the poverty level, and were in need of some type of social service.[8]

Most undocumented Mexican aliens congregate in *barrios* scattered throughout Southern California, where the Mexican culture remains intact. According to Baca and Bryan's study of the attitudes of undocumented Mexican aliens living in Los Angeles, the vast majority of undocumented aliens would like the right to cross the border legally to work.[9] They expressed loyalty to their homeland and considered themselves to be binational. They desired a set of residency rights that would protect them from the indignities and hazards of their second-class status.

Practice Articles

The author reviewed articles on Mexican Americans that appeared in *Social Casework* and *Social Work* from January 1964 to May 1983 to determine whether they included information on practice

Table 1.

Major Themes of Articles on Mexican Americans in the Social Work Literature (N = 21)

Themes	Number of Articles
Cultural differences and the need for social justice	6
Importance of language	1
Human relations skills	2
Experiences with racism and the need for social justice	8
The Mexican-American family	4

that can be used to help undocumented aliens.[10] In general, most of the twenty-one articles reviewed by the author were concerned with the racism experienced by Mexican Americans, the need for social justice, and the cultural differences between Anglos and Mexican Americans. Table 1 shows that cultural differences and the experiences of racism are the most frequent topics discussed in the literature.

Only a few articles elaborated on the type of knowledge that social workers need to work effectively with Mexican Americans. For instance, Sotomayor illustrated how systems theory can be used to analyze the relationship of Mexican-American families in the *barrio* to subsystems outside the *barrio*.[11] Santa Cruz and Hepworth reported a study of clients' perceptions of the helping relationship formed with social workers of a different ethnic background.[12] They concluded that both Anglo and Mexican-American clients were positive about these initial helping relationships; however, all the Mexican Americans were bilingual and bicultural, and all who spoke only Spanish were excluded from the sample. Only four articles gave specific suggestions on how to work with Mexican Americans, but they offered no frameworks for practice.[13] Just one article described a study on the use of services by undocumented Mexican aliens and recommended reforms in immigration policies.[14]

Although the articles are limited in their frameworks for practice, they are useful in identifying issues such as racism that are areas for intervention with undocumented aliens. However, the incorporation of these issues is difficult partially because of the conceptual constraints imposed by social work practice theory. According to Nelsen, social workers perceive phenomena exclusively and narrowly through the method in which they have been trained.[15] And, as Meyer pointed out, owing to the methods framework, social work continues to ignore what has to be done about broader social problems.[16] The profession's efforts to develop new forms of practice have not included a consideration of the impact of economic and political forces on the needs of individuals. Because of the Reagan Administration's policies and the conservative political climate in this society, social work has been leaning toward an emphasis on clinical practice rather than attacking such problems as racism through other approaches.

Political Approach

If the profession wants to adopt new forms of practice, then the question becomes, What other practice knowledge is needed to address the problems of undocumented Mexican aliens? Social work practice has been defined as a "professionally guided system that engages people and their social units in change activities to alter their psychosocial functioning for the purpose of improving the quality of life."[17] It occurs with individuals, families, small groups, organizations, and communities. As Morales noted:

> Social work intervention might be directed at the person, the environment, or both. In each case, the social worker seeks to enhance and restore the social functioning of people or to change social conditions that impede the mutually beneficial interaction between people and their environment.[18]

Social work practice becomes political when the practitioner and the client seek to accommodate, through influence, pressure, and negotiation, a just distribution of resources or services from the environment. The skills needed by social workers in political activities are "knowledge of the political 'setup' of each problem-solving situation," "ability to discover the common interests—the problem—of the participants," "assistance in negotiating a solution," and "support for a plan of action."[19]

Social workers need to practice a series of political skills if they are to intervene effectively with or for undocumented aliens. At no time in history have social workers encountered more controversy regarding undocumented aliens from Mexico, as well as refugees from other countries, than in the 1980s. Not to participate in political action against the oppressive conditions faced by this group is tantamount to acceding to those negative political conditions. Alexander provided the following rationale for political practice in his discussion of the importance of political responsibility in professional practice:

> Mastering the social work role and responsibility to enhance the interaction between the individual and society, including that portion of this role which involves the political process, promises to produce a quantum leap forward in the impact the profession has and in the recognition it receives. Intelligent advocacy, based on objective policies of the profession, will bring social workers into legislative and decision-making bodies as constituents, consultants, and elected participants. . . . [20]

As social workers begin to take a political approach to the provision of services for undocumented aliens, it will be necessary to make explicit the profession's value stance of working for justice and of the importance of human rights to establish a rationale for action. Social work practice has concentrated on the concept of needs rather than rights. However, the needs of undocumented aliens cannot be met until the following barriers are eliminated: the lack of resources, inequitable immigration laws, discriminatory practices, exploitation by employers, and fraudulent contracts. Therefore, if social workers are to be successful with these people, they must establish intervention strategies that promote rights as well as needs and adopt an aggressive stance on advocacy.

INTERVENTION STRATEGIES

As was already mentioned, the goal of social work is to help persons resolve problems that are related to social functioning, including problems in themselves and with other significant persons. This approach is called direct service. Much has been written on this type of intervention, and social workers are well prepared to assist clients with their psychological needs. Intervention on behalf of clients with such organizational structures as the Immigration and Naturalization Service, the courts, and welfare institutions may be referred to as indirect service. In working with undocumented aliens who are often prey to deportation, arrests, and economic exploitation, social workers should practice indirect intervention if they are to be as effective as possible.

Political strategies can be initiated in anticipation of social problems. They include such activities as advocacy, class-action advocacy, and social reform. According to Brager:

> The [social] worker as advocate identifies with the plight of the disadvantaged. He sees as his primary responsibility the tough-minded and partisan representation of their interest, and this supersedes his fealty to others. This role inevitably requires that the practitioner function as a political tactician.[21]

The NASW Ad Hoc Committee on Advocacy quoted two definitions of *advocate*: "one that pleads the cause of another" and "one who argues for, defends, maintains, or recommends a cause or a proposal."[22] In this article, the author uses the second definition because it "incorporates the political meaning ascribed to the word in which the interests of a class of people [undocumented aliens] are represented."[23] Advocacy in behalf of a powerless population such as undocumented aliens is appropriate practice in that it involves representing the interests of a disenfranchised class. To help undocumented aliens through advocacy, social service agencies should employ bilingual, bicultural social workers. This type of social worker could use his or her knowledge of Spanish and political skills to become the client's support system, translator, adviser, and defender and hence could represent the Spanish-speaking alien and negotiate needed services.

Class-action advocacy is another potential arena for political practice. Social workers could engage in class-action advocacy to improve the well-being and to protect the rights of undocumented aliens. According to Morales, "class action is a legal concept that has promising implications for social work."[24] Both bilingual and English-speaking social workers would work with other professionals and with a legal agency to "translate [humanitarian] concerns into legal class action suits."[25] Winning in the courts could establish the right to services of undocumented aliens.

An example of class-action advocacy was the actions of social workers and health professionals employed by the Los Angeles County Health Alliance (as well as union members and undocumented aliens) in behalf of undocumented aliens. The alliance, in conjunction with the Western Center on Law and Poverty—a legal agency—filed suit against the Los Angeles County Health Department. Social workers and other professionals filed declarations that resulted in a court order forbidding the health department from requiring undocumented aliens to sign up for Medi-Cal as a condition for obtaining health services. If the undocumented aliens had applied for Medi-Cal, their names would have been sent to the Immigration and Naturalization Service.[26]

The opportunity to build coalitions for social reform by English-speaking and bilingual social workers and other interested groups is another promising approach. According to Rothman, "social reform involves activity by a coalition of interests which acts vigorously on behalf of some client group which is at risk or disadvantaged."[27] Coalition building for social reform can be successful if there is broad public support, although it requires considerable effort to convince specific groups that they should participate. It has been used by groups in the *barrio* to fight mass deportations, the forced sterilization of undocumented alien women, and the withdrawal or refusal of health care that was just described.[28]

CONCLUSION

The NASW Minority Affairs Conference issued a statement condemning the racist policies and practices of the Immigration and Naturalization Service against Haitian refugees and undocumented aliens. Unlike other professions, social work must continue to recognize the existence of undocumented aliens—a disenfranchised class of people who share a common oppression of economic exploitation as other third-world minorities of color.

This article pointed out that the clinical practice method is too narrow to be effective with undocumented aliens and introduced the concept of a political approach that allows for indirect advocacy to help undocumented aliens gain their rights and fulfill their needs. The proposed interventions also can be useful with other immigrant groups, such as Vietnamese and Haitian refugees.

The following recommendations are offered in the hope that they will contribute to the creation of a policy that is humane and just:

1. Undocumented aliens and their families who are residing in the United States should be granted amnesty. The current policy is to deport them to their country of origin—an approach that only creates undue hardships for them.

2. Undocumented alien families with children should be eligible for some form of public assistance. The social welfare system must address itself to the needs of this deprived group.

3. Social work services should be offered to undocumented aliens utilizing the framework and approach described in this article. The problems of these aliens should be of concern to social work.

Notes and References

1. Ramón M. Salcido, "Undocumented Aliens: A Study of Mexican Families," *Social Work*, 24 (July 1979), p. 306.
2. Wayne A. Cornelius, *Illegal Mexican Migration to the United States* (Cambridge, Mass.: MIT Press, 1977).
3. Wayne A. Cornelius et al., *Mexican Immigrants and Southern California: A Summary of Current Knowledge*, Research Report Series (San Diego: Center for U.S.–Mexican Studies, University of California at San Diego, 1982), p. 54.
4. See Whitney W. Hicks, "Economic Development and Fertility Change in Mexico," *Demography*, 1 (August 1974), pp. 407–421; and Leo Grebler, "Mexican-American Study Project," Advance Report 2 (Los Angeles: Division of Research, Graduate School of Business Administration, University of California, 1965).
5. Tim W. Dagadag, "Source Regions and Composition of Illegal Mexican Immigration to California," *International Migration Review*, 9 (Winter 1975), pp. 499–510.
6. Parker Frisbe, "Illegal Migration from Mexico to the United States: A Longitudinal Analysis," *International Migration Review*, 9 (Spring 1975), pp. 3–15.
7. Julian Samora, ed., *Los Mojados: The Wetback Story* (Notre Dame, Ind.: University of Notre Dame Press, 1971).
8. Ramón M. Salcido, "Utilization of Community and Immigration Experiences of Documented and Undocumented Mexican Families." Unpublished doctoral dissertation, University of California, Los Angeles, 1977.
9. Evan Maxwell, "Most Illegal Aliens Don't Want to Stay in U.S., Study Indicates," *Los Angeles Times*, July 16, 1980, p. 1.
10. Lydia R. Aguirre, "The Meaning of the Chicano Movement," pp. 259–261, Tomás C. Antencio, "The Survival of La Raza Despite Social Services," pp. 262–268, John Florez, "Chicanos and Coalitions as a Force for Social Change," pp. 269–273, Alejandro Garcia, "The Chicano and Social Work," pp. 274–278, Faustina Ramirez Knoll, "Casework Services for Mexican Americans," pp. 279–284, Armando Morales, "The Collective Preconscious and Racism," pp. 285–293, Phillip D. Ortego, "The Chicano Renaissance," pp. 294–307, Faustina Solis, "Socioeconomic and Cultural Conditions of Migrant Workers," pp. 308–315, and Marta Sotomayor, "Mexican-American Interaction with Social Systems," pp. 316–322, all in *Social Casework*, 52 (May 1971). See also Ignacio Aguilar, "Initial Contacts with Mexican-American Families," *Social Work*, 17 (May 1972), pp. 66–70; Miguel Montiel, "The Chicano Family: A Review of Research," *Social Work*, 18 (March 1973), pp. 22–31; Renaldo J. Maduro and Carlos F. Martinez, "Latino Dream Analysis: Opportunity for Confrontation," *Social Casework*, 55 (October 1974), pp. 461–469; Luciano A. Santa Cruz and Dean H. Hepworth, "News and Views: Effects of Cultural Orientation on Casework," *Social Casework*, 56 (January 1975), pp. 52–57; Teresa Ramirez Boulette, "Group Therapy with Low-Income Mexican Americans," *Social Work*, 20 (September 1975), pp. 403–405; David Maldonado, Jr., "The Chicano Aged," *Social Work*, 20 (May 1975), pp. 213–216; Aguilar and Virginia N. Wood, "Therapy through a Death Ritual," *Social Work*, 21 (January 1976), pp. 49–54; Celia Medina and Maria R. Reyes, "Dilemmas of Chicana Counselors," *Social Work*, 21 (November 1976), pp. 515–517; Henry Ebihara, "A Training Program for Bilingual Paraprofessionals," *Social Casework*, 60 (May 1979), pp. 274–281; Ramón M. Salcido, "Undocumented Aliens: A Study of Mexican Families," *Social Work*, 24 (July 1979), pp. 306–311; Salcido, "Problems of the Mexican-American Elderly

in an Urban Setting," *Social Casework*, 60 (December 1979), pp. 609–615; and Ted R. Watkins and Richard Gonzales, "Outreach to Mexican Americans," *Social Work*, 27 (January 1982), pp. 68–73.

11. Sotomayor, "Mexican American Interaction with Social Systems."

12. Santa Cruz and Hepworth, "News and Views."

13. Knoll, "Casework Services for Mexican Americans"; Aguilar, "Initial Contacts with Mexican American Families"; Boulette, "Group Therapy with Low-Income Mexican Americans"; and Watkins and Gonzales, "Outreach to Mexican Americans."

14. Salcido, "Undocumented Aliens."

15. Judith C. Nelsen, "Social Work's Fields of Practice, Methods, and Models: The Choice to Act," *Social Service Review*, 49 (June 1975), pp. 264–270.

16. Carol H. Meyer, "What Directions for Direct Practice?" *Social Work*, 24 (July 1979), pp. 267–272.

17. Chauncey A. Alexander, "Social Work Practice: A Unitary Conception," *Social Work*, 22 (September 1977), p. 413. See also Alexander, "Professional Social Workers and Political Responsibility," in Maryann Mahaffey and John W. Hanks, eds., *Practical Politics: Social Work and Political Responsibility* (Silver Spring, Md.: National Association of Social Workers, 1982), pp. 15–31.

18. Armando Morales, "Social Work with Third-World People," *Social Work*, 26 (January 1981), p. 46.

19. Allison D. Murdach, "A Political Perspective in Problem Solving," *Social Work*, 27 (September 1982), p. 418.

20. Alexander, "Professional Social Workers and Political Responsibility," p. 31.

21. George A. Brager, "Advocacy and Political Behavior," *Social Work*, 13 (April 1968), p. 6.

22. Ad Hoc Committee on Advocacy, "The Social Worker as Advocate: Champion of Social Victims," *Social Work*, 14 (April 1969), pp. 16–19.

23. Ibid., p. 17.

24. Armando Morales, "Social Work with Third-World People," p. 49.

25. Ibid.

26. "Plan Bars Free Care for Aliens," *Daily Breeze*, March 29, 1983, Part 1, p. 8.

27. Jack Rothman, "Three Models of Community Organization Practice, Their Mixing and Phasing," in Fred M. Cox et al., *Strategies of Community Organization* (Itasca, Ill.: F. E. Peacock Publishers, 1979), pp. 41–42.

28. "A Report on Latin American Immigration," *La Gente de Aztlan* (February 1982), p. 7.

Racial and Personal Identity in the Black Experience

Leon W. Chestang

Establishing a sense of identity is a basic human need. The essence of this phenomenon, according to Erikson, is a sense of stability and continuity of the self.[1] In addition to a myriad of life experiences, a person's achievements represent a major component of his or her identity. This last point is significant in understanding the experiences of black Americans in establishing a sense of identity because of the limited opportunities available to them. In spite of the limitations, black Americans have established a firm sense of their identity. Because of these limitations and related circumstances, their identity has a special character whose key aspect is racial identity.

This article traces the process and dynamics of identity formation among a group of black Americans. Its thesis is that the maintenance of dignity is at the center of the black person's quest for identity and that two elements are involved in the process: (1) achieving success and (2) developing a sense of identity, including the establishment of a personal identity and identification with one's race.

The formulations presented in the article are based on the author's analysis of the lives of twenty black Americans, both male and female, from all regions of the United States.[2] These twenty people lived at various periods of history, from the mid-1800s to the present. This article presents an account of the experiences of eleven of the twenty people—Marian Anderson, Maya Angelou, James Baldwin, Angela Davis, Ralph Ellison, Lorraine Hansberry, Lena Horne, Malcolm X, Gordon Parks, Jackie Robinson, and Ethel Waters—whom the author considers to be representative of them all. The formulations are not considered final, but they suggest an approach to understanding how black Americans experience identity formation.

ACHIEVING SUCCESS

The path to success often was discouraging and demanding for most of the twenty people. Yet they chose a particular path because of their socialization, especially the sense of pride, self-respect, and hope for the future that was laid down in their early interactions with their families. Their socialization, in combination with the aid of social intervenors, acted to counterbalance the social forces that impinged on their orientation to achievement and spurred them to continue in a given direction. For these individuals, then, becoming successful represented the fulfillment of the promise of their socialization. To be sure, they did not eschew the social and personal rewards of success, such as recognition, status, and material benefits, that are sought by most people. However, in the context of their status as black people, what deserves emphasis was that becoming successful also was a behavioral declaration of their dignity. This latter meaning of success is particularly important for understanding the dimensions contributed by race to the motivation to achieve.

Struggle Against the Obstacles to Success

One requirement that these people faced on the path to achievement was the struggle against the obstacles to success—primarily limited financial means and racial prejudice. They frequently encountered rejection, taunts, racial slurs, and humiliation. The methods they used to deal with these obstacles varied according to the situation and the personality of the individual.

Enduring Abuse. Among the most common means of dealing with the insults and other forms of personal deprecation related to racial prejudice was *enduring abuse*—the subordination of personal feelings to the pursuit of one's goals. This style of coping is illustrated in Parks's response to being insulted by his employer after he complained about being fed leftovers or scraps from customers' plates:

> He called me a liar and threatened to fire me. In spite of my hunger, I dumped the food into the garbage and finished my chores. Then later, while his back was turned, I slipped four raw wieners and a container of milk into my pockets. In answer to my "Goodnight," he...snarled,

"Go to hell!" I wanted to quit, then and there; but common sense buttoned my lips. And I left without another word.[3]

Anderson reacted in a similar way on being told by the receptionist that the music school to which she was applying did not accept Negroes (what black people were called at that time):

> I just looked at this girl and was as shocked that such words could come from one so young. . . .I could not conceive of a person surrounded as she was with the joy of music without having some sense of its beauty and understanding rub off on her. I did not argue with her or ask to see her superior. It was as if a cold and horrifying hand had been laid on me. I turned and walked out.[4]

This author has suggested elsewhere that the necessity to respond in the manner just described requires "the development of ego-syntonic modes that are often at variance with the personality trends considered normal by the majority group."[5] When these modes, necessitated by the social context, are integrated into the personality, behaviors usually considered antisocial or wrong become justifiable and valid from the perspective of the actor.[6] In this process, the person redefines or reinterprets the situation and thus alters his or her relationship with the environment. The situational context is altered, and behaviors that have one meaning in the context of the wider society may have a different meaning to the minority person. Parks's pragmatic behavior in stuffing four weiners and a container of milk into his pockets when his employer's back was turned is a case in point.

Forbearance. Another form of coping results from an attitude that can be characterized as *forbearance,* which suggests the qualities of fortitude and self-control under provocation. This capacity stems both from common sense and a sense of personal dignity. It is reflected in Robinson's hard fight against "loneliness and abuse. . .[and his denial] of his true feelings so that the 'noble experiment' [becoming the first black in professional baseball] could succeed."[7] It was more powerfully expressed, however, in Angelou's description of her grandmother's reaction to a display of disrespect, taunting, and impudence by a group of white teenage girls who confronted her grandmother for the express purpose of humiliating her. Angelou's grandmother stood and watched as one girl, without undergarments, raised her dress before this highly religious, elderly woman, who calmly hummed a spiritual as she regarded them. As Angelou described it:

She stood another whole song through and then opened the screen door to look down on me cry—in rage. She looked until I looked up. Her face was a brown moon that shone on me. She was beautiful. Something had happened out there which I couldn't completely understand but I could see that she was happy. Then she bent down and touched me as mothers of the Church "lay hands on the sick and afflicted," and I was calmed.

"Go wash your face, Sister," and she went behind the candy counter and hummed, "Glory, glory, hallelujah, when I lay my burden down."

I threw the well water on my face and used the weekday handkerchief to blow my nose. Whatever the contest had been out front, I knew Mama had won.[8]

Perseverance. Another way of coping, shown by the twenty people in their quest for success, is *perseverance*. Perseverance refers to the tenacity of will and the dedication to purpose in spite of hardships. It can be considered the behavioral component of the attitude of forbearance in that forbearance represents a way of feeling, and perseverance represents a way of being; thus, forbearance is passive, but perseverance is active. Perseverance was usually triggered by a denial of opportunity or a challenge to the person's ability, and it was aimed at demonstrating that one could succeed at whatever had been denied or challenged. It is illustrated by Parks's behavior during a period when he was without money and had repeatedly been denied employment:

So I hung on, preying upon waste receptacles for newspapers that carried the daily ads. And I answered them. But it was always my "youth" or some other fabricated excuse that disqualified me. I hunted for the warm spots where there was light so that I could work on new lyrics and melodies. . .and the futility of those days was so well reflected in those lyrics and songs my friends began to call me "Blue." Every line in that notebook spoke of heartbreak and hard luck.[9]

From this description, it is clear that persisting at an apparently impossible task is an integral part of the capacity to achieve.

Proving One's Competence

A second requirement that these black persons faced in their quest to achieve was their need to disprove the prevailing stereotype of the inability and incompetence of black people. Thus, *proving their competence* was another way that they met assaults on their dignity. This style of coping involved going to great lengths to show that they were capable of the task in question. Such extensions of the self have resulted, in some cases, in the judgment that the black person who succeeds in some endeavor has done so because he or she is an overachiever or is exceptional. The notion of the overachiever, which suggests that the person's behavior has a questionable psychological foundation, does not, however, parallel the idea of proving competence. Whereas the concept of overachievement points to the high personal and psychological costs of the behavior, proving competence points to the excessive social demands on black persons to show repeatedly not only that they are adequate but that they are superior in their chosen endeavor. From the perspective of black people, it also points to the demand that they must undertake unusual routes involving personal sacrifice and the extension of the self. The personal sacrifice and extension of self required by taking these routes, it should be remembered, are not voluntary but are consequences of the socially imposed restrictions on opportunity and mobility. This style of coping is manifested in Malcolm X's reaction to being told by his white high school teacher that it was impossible for him to become a lawyer or other professional: "Whatever I have done since then, I have driven myself to become a success at it."[10] It also is seen in Anderson's decision to give up a blossoming career in the United States to spend several years in Europe to learn the languages in which the songs she sang were written.[11] It is exemplified by the persistent efforts of Robinson to be flawless on the playing field because he knew that "any mistake. . .would be magnified because [he] was the only black man out there."[12]

The twenty people used a variety of self-protective maneuvers to shield themselves from assaults on their dignity. Some of these maneuvers were in the active mode, and some were passive. In either case, however, the goal of the behavior was to maintain their dignity. Davis described one form the active mode can take:

> We developed our own means of defending our egos. Our weapon was the word. We would gather on my front lawn, wait for a car of white people to pass by and shout the worst epithets for white people we knew: Cracker, Redneck. Then we would laugh hysterically at the startled expression on their faces. I hid this pastime from my parents. They could not know how important it was for me and for all of us who had just discovered racism, to find ways of maintaining our dignity.[13]

Horne's response to the curiosity of white people about her as a black performer exemplifies how some blacks build a wall between themselves and whites to avoid being hurt. Thus, Horne decided at one point in her career to give white audiences an image of herself as "a woman they could not reach....They got the singer, but not the woman."[14]

DEVELOPING A SENSE OF IDENTITY

Erikson defined identity as "a sense of personal sameness and historical continuity."[15] He meant that identity is a stabilizing force in the personality which gives the feeling that while life and one's experiences change, each new experience becomes integrated with one's existing identity. Thus, the fundamental self-representation remains intact, although elaborated. The sense of historical continuity is linked to this idea and suggests that one's past, when validated by present actions congenial to one's society, gives one confidence for the future. Past, present, and future are interrelated in that the internalized past is the foundation for present actions and the promise of a future.

The concept of identity played a critical role in the maintenance and the assertion of dignity by the people whose lives were examined, and the role of identity operated on two levels—racial identity and personal identity. These persons were confronted with a host of negative identities involving attributions of inferiority and incompetence. It would have been contrary to all accepted principles of human development for such experiences not to have affected their functioning. Indeed, the discussion up to this point has shown that the experiences leading to these negative identities played a vital role in shaping behavior. However, the negative experiences were met with other experiences and actions of a more positive nature, which also had an effect; the result was that both negative and positive experiences became aspects of these persons' identity.

The negative experiences and the process of grappling with them are the essentials of racial identity. Although, as was just implied, racial identity and personal identity are interrelated, they are discussed separately in this article for heuristic purposes and because it is important to show the different roles played by these two aspects of identity in maintaining a sense of dignity.

Racial Identity

Racial identity refers to the identification with the alienation, social differentiation, and deprecation that these people and members of their race experienced in their contact with the wider society. Equally important, it refers to more gratifying experiences that resulted from transactions and encounters with members of their own group. Because the effects just cited are due to one's membership in a particular group (black people), they heighten one's awareness of the group's plight and hence one's consciousness of race. Thus, being black becomes something that one is and a group to which one belongs. On a personal level, this fact leads to a psychological cohesion (identification) with others who share membership in one's group.

Among the principal elements involved in the group cohesion that is reflected in racial identification are exclusion from and rejection by the wider society. Confronted by these forces, the persons under consideration turned to their own group for support and self-esteem. Thus, from their perspectives, the two groups—black and white—are juxtaposed, with their own group being defined as "good" and whites being viewed as "evil." This juxtaposing of the two groups and the related defining processes involve most aspects of life, but especially cultural patterns and lifestyles. Moreover, the ability to cope with the forces that necessitated the juxtaposition become sources of pride and self-esteem. A comment by Waters is pertinent in this regard:

> I have the soundest of reasons for being proud of my people. We Negroes have always had such a tough time that our very survival in this white world with the dice always loaded against us is the greatest possible testimonial to our strength, our courage, and our immunity to adversity.[16]

In describing the ambiance of the black community, Angelou showed this pride in another way:

> In the evenings on the way home the sensations were joy, anticipation and relief at the first sign which said Barbecue or Do Drop Inn or Home Cooking or at the first brown faces on the streets. I recognized that I was again in my country.[17]

Achieving Personal Identity

In asserting their dignity, achievement-oriented persons reach beyond racial pride and seek to establish a sense of personal identity. Thus, the twenty people worked to acquire a view of themselves that transcended race and which established them as unique individuals. For them, race was only one aspect of their identity, albeit an important one. Their complexity as individuals and the assertion of their right to individuality were the main elements in the process of establishing personal identity. These two elements are, of course, interrelated, the one emphasizing the multidimensional quality of the person and the other emphasizing his or her singularity.

Baldwin commented on "the immensity and the variety of experience called Negro. . .[and expressed the view] that one should recognize this variety as wealth."[18] This point has been explicit throughout the article, and it is exemplified in the lives of the people under study. These people came from a variety of backgrounds; they were from different regions and social classes and had various vocational and career interests. Although, as this article has shown, they all had to cope with a common set of social circumstances imposed by their race, their particular styles of coping reflected the variety of their backgrounds and their complexity as individuals. In calling for recognition of their complexity as individuals, the subjects expressed the human desire not to be viewed in what Erikson called a "totalistic" fashion.[19] This is to say that they were rejecting the stereotypic idea that blacks can be defined and understood by their race alone. That most of the people expressed pride in their race but also sought achievement in the context of the wider society is not contradictory. In showing both these motivations, they were behaving in accord with the reality of their existence: They were both black and American. Ellison spoke to this point in discussing how he came to terms with his complexity. He said: "I was forced, thus, to relate myself consciously and imaginatively to my mixed background as American, as Negro American, and as a Negro from what was in its own belated way a pioneer background."[20] Again, in calling for recognition of the complexity of the black experience, these persons were not surrendering their racial identity. Instead, they were seeking a fuller identity— one that would reflect more accurately the multidimensional quality of their personal experience. Ellison offered the following explanation:

> As a kid, I remember working it out this way: there was a world in which you wore your every-day clothes on Sunday, and there was a world in which you wore your Sunday clothes every day. I wanted the world in which you wore your Sunday clothes every day. I wanted it because it represented something better, a more exciting and civilized and human way of living.[21]

But compare his explanation of his craft in the following extract:

> As for my writer's necessity of cashing in on the pain undergone by
> my people (and remember I write of the humor as well), writing is
> my way of confronting, often for the hundredth time, that same pain
> and that same pleasure. It is my way of seeing that it not be in vain.[22]

In these two quotations, one sees how the desire for achievement
and consciousness of race can exist side by side. One also sees
in bold relief the nature of the complexity that was referred to
before. It is the human complexity of having many-faceted motivations, all congruent and all pointing toward the same goal—the
maintenance of dignity.

The subjects' claim to the right to individuality was the final
step in the assertion of their dignity. It involved projecting their
uniqueness as individuals and acting in accord with that projec-
tion. Although the development of consciousness of race involved
the group, the struggle to establish a personal identity was carried
out alone. Contemplation and introspection were the hallmarks of
this process, which culminated in the calm, self-confidence of being at home in oneself. At the same time, the behaviors that reflected
this state of being were, of course, performed in relation to others,
both black and white. The process through which these people
developed a sense of personal identity, however, deserves further
elaboration.

Challenging and rejecting imposed definitions of themselves and
refusing to yield to external pressures for conformity were key aspects
of the process of establishing personal identity. These key aspects
represented a kind of self-assertiveness that was uncommon in their
experience. As such, self-assertiveness reflected the first expressions
of active choice and personal autonomy. Thus, it was both an anti-
dote to the impotence often felt by blacks and a contributor to
self-esteem. It is noteworthy that the process of challenging and
rejecting imposed definitions of themselves related to transactions
with members of their own race as well as with whites. As Ellison
noted:

> I learned that nothing could go unchallenged; especially that feverish
> industry dedicated to telling Negroes who and what they are, and which
> can usually be counted upon to deprive both humanity and culture
> of their complexity.[23]

Horne discussed another facet of this idea in explaining her desire
to be seen and to respond as an individual. She recognized that
she had been a symbol of the "good Negro" for years, and that

this image had paid off for her personally and financially. At the same time, seeing that the racial situation of blacks in general had not changed, she wanted to work in the civil rights movement. She insisted, however, that her actions for the causes of blacks were to be motivated by her own desires and personal style.

> I wanted to re-identify myself with the Negro people. And yet I did not want to be forced into it, by some organization, by some external pressure. I wanted it to be an act of my own choosing. Involvement of this kind implies the right to choose non-involvement sometimes too.[24]

Establishing a sense of personal identity not only was a matter of challenging and rejecting external definitions, but implied achievement in some area, such as social activism or a career. Erikson discussed in detail the import of this aspect of personal identity.[25] Here, it is sufficient to reiterate the idea that because achievement is among the most crucial avenues to identity for Americans in general, it is understandable that it is central to the identity of blacks. Hansberry corroborated this point in responding to a inquiry about her response to success:

> It probably is the most fulfilling experience a human being can have—to try to create something and to have it received with any measure of recognition for the effort. So that I can only say it in personal terms: I get an enormous sense of personal fulfillment—a slight sense of justification for being.[26]

From this quotation, it can be seen that the search for dignity and the search for personal identity converge. They are reciprocals, each supporting the other. An insult to dignity is a threat to personal identity; a challenge to personal identity questions dignity. Thus, the establishment of a sense of personal identity assumes a high importance in the overall search for dignity, and it is the culmination and the epitome of the functionality of achievement.

IMPLICATIONS FOR PRACTICE

Questions about and issues of black identity, so frequently raised during the 1960s and 1970s, continue to be discussed in the 1980s. Many discussions of this important subject fail to distinguish between racial and personal identity. This failure has caused much confusion and many problems for people who experience conflicts in this area.

Whether they are dealing with black adolescents, young adults, or older persons, it is imperative that social workers be clear about the issues involved in racial and personal identity. These issues have major consequences for problems associated with the development of adolescents, their achievement in school, and their romantic relationships and marriage. The effects of the failure to deal with these issues is seen also in the personal adjustment and work adjustment of individuals.

On the basis of his examination of the lives of twenty black Americans and the theory and research on this subject, the author suggested some crucial components of racial and personal identity. Instead of seeing individuality as a fault, social workers, teachers, and others should view it as a strength and a positive step. Black youths should be encouraged to express their uniqueness, which can serve as a control on the negative influences of peer groups. Young adults should be helped to assert their individuality, which can lessen the tendency to try to control their friends, lovers, spouses, or children. Being confident of their identity may prevent a host of interpersonal problems that the clients of social workers experience.

Notes and References

1. Erik H. Erikson, *Childhood and Society* (2d ed.; New York: W. W. Norton & Co., 1963).

2. Data for this article were taken from a major study entitled "Achievement and Self-Esteem among Black Americans: A Study of 20 Lives," unpublished Ph.D. thesis, School of Social Service Administration, University of Chicago, 1977. An earlier article that analyzed factors associated with black Americans' achievement of success appears in Martin Bloom, *Life Span Development* (New York: Macmillan Publishing Co., 1980).

3. Gordon Parks, *A Choice of Weapons* (New York: Harper & Row, 1965), p. 23.

4. Marian Anderson, *My Lord, What a Morning* (New York: Avon Books, 1956).

5. Leon W. Chestang, *Character Development in a Hostile Environment*, Occasional Paper No. 3 (Chicago: School of Social Service Administration, University of Chicago), p. 7.

6. See Robert Merton, *Social Theory and Social Structure* (rev. ed.; Glencoe, Ill.: Free Press, 1957), pp. 187–188, for a detailed explication of this point as it applies to more general situations.

7. Jackie Robinson, as told to Al Duckett, *I Never Had It Made* (New York: J. P. Putnam's Sons, 1972), p. 256.

8. Maya Angelou, *I Know Why the Caged Bird Sings* (New York: Random House, 1970), pp. 26–27.

9. Parks, *A Choice of Weapons*, p. 39.

10. *The Autobiography of Malcolm X*, Alex Haley, ed. (New York: Grove Press, 1966), p. 38.

11. Anderson, *My Lord, What a Morning*.

12. See Robinson, *I Never Had It Made*, p. 256. The reactive quality of the subjects' responses is understandable, for there is a social component to every act. George H. Mead addressed this point in *Mind, Self and Society: From the Standpoint of a Social Behaviorist* (Chicago: University of Chicago Press, 1934), pp. 175–176.

13. Angela Davis, *Angela Davis: An Autobiography* (New York: Random House, 1974), p. 80.

14. Lena Horne and Richard Scheckel, *Lena* (New York: New American Library, 1966), pp. 149–150.

15. Erikson, *Childhood and Society*, p. 17.

16. Ethel Waters, *His Eye Is on the Sparrow* (New York: Bantam Books, 1952), p. 92.

17. Angelou, *I Know Why the Caged Bird Sings*, p. 192.

18. James Baldwin, *Nobody Knows My Name* (New York: Dell Publishing Co., 1972), pp. 44–45.

19. Erikson, *Childhood and Society*.

20. Ralph Ellison, *Shadow and Act* (New York: Random House, 1966; originally published in 1953), p. xvi.

21. Ibid., p. 25.

22. Ibid., p. 41.

23. Ibid., p. xvii.

24. Horne, *Lena*, pp. 205–206.

25. Erikson, *Childhood and Society*.

26. Lorraine Hansberry, *To Be Young, Gifted and Black: Lorraine Hansberry in Her Own Words*, Robert Nemiroff, ed. (New York: New American Library, 1970), p. 126.

Black Sex-Role Research:
Some Uses and Abuses of Data

Dorothy M. Linder

The topic of black sex roles is so intertwined with "color" in a white society that it is difficult to consider one without the other. Color is a primary factor in understanding the constellation of qualities that characterize black men and women in Western society. As long as society draws distinctions along color lines, color will continue to be a critical dimension. The circular nature of theory, research, and practice related to race is addressed in this article because effective and efficient practice with black families demands more than a desire to help or the fact of being born into the same ethnic group as a client.[1] The beliefs that black people and white people have of each other, based on color, influence the ability of both groups to communicate. For example, white people frequently label black people as immoral, lazy, violent, and mentally deficient, whereas black people often perceive white people to be pushy, arrogant, dumb, and stealthy. Such stereotypical thinking is acquired early in one's socialization and reinforced by many environmental forces.[2] Particularly, stereotyping along racial lines can lead to improper assessment and intervention strategies.

BACKGROUND

Although the topic of sex roles has generated widespread interest, there has been little consensus on the social roles of black men, women, and children. Research has produced inconsistent findings in such areas as racial differences in child rearing,[3] the psychological adjustment characteristics of female heads of households,[4] whether egalitarianism is a distinctive conjugal role pattern in black families,[5] and the effects of the father's absence on children.[6] Thus, it is difficult to discern if major advances have occurred in this area of knowledge. This article attempts to examine the substantive concerns of research on black sex roles and their important links to practice and policy. Such an exposition is needed because of the recurring enormity of research violations that have given rise to inconsistencies in data. These violations, although not necessarily intentional, frequently are the result of investigators' biases regarding sex and race.

The uses and abuses cited in this article are illustrative, not exhaustive, owing to space limitations. Thus, the author will report on selective characteristics of research on black sex roles and on the general character of that research in the past few decades. The objectives, theoretical formulations, sampling procedures, methodologies, findings, and conclusions of the various studies will be discussed, although the major focus will be on the conceptual bases of this research because the author believes that the initial stage of research profoundly affects the direction of the remaining investigation.

To connect the universal aspects of the socialization to sex roles with the literature on black families, the author conducted an extensive review of the literature on racial differences in child rearing, family role performance, socialization patterns, and effects of these patterns on children—four topics that are representative of the general body of research on black sex roles.[7] The reader is reminded that although this article emphasizes research on black families, the issues and implications for practice and policy making are relevant to other families, individuals, and groups as well.

The uses and abuses discussed in this article should alert the reader to the pitfalls of research in this area, stimulate research that has utility for practice, and enable social workers to assess realistically the dilemmas faced by their black clients.

DEFINITIONS AND THEORETICAL FORMULATIONS

The term "sex role" has been used to refer to sexual stratification, to the assignment of tasks in society and in the family, and to the preferences for behavioral arrangements between the sexes.[8] It has been characterized as a general role that interacts with other social roles, such as student or athlete, and with age to produce an age-sex structure that includes infant, boy, girl, young man, young woman, old man, and old woman.[9] Sex role is a patterned phenomenon that is best understood in the context of its interactions with other social roles, statuses, and codes defining lineage and kinship.[10] Block defined it as a constellation of qualities that an individual understands to characterize males and females in a specific culture.[11]

"Black sex roles" thus are defined as the constellation of qualities understood to characterize the social roles of black males and females in American culture. Specifically, they are clearly set apart from the conventional classification of sex roles by racial and social class distinctions.

Theoretical Background

The classical theoretical formulations underlying a person's socialization to sex roles are Freudian identification, cognitive development, social learning, and social power. All the formulations stress that identification with these roles occurs in childhood and that this early identification is vital in explaining the behavior of adults.[12]

Freudian psychoanalytic theory. Freudian theory assumes that all persons pass through a set sequence of stages of psychosexual development. Children of both sexes initially identify with the primary love object, "mother," as she is associated with oral and anal activities. The three most important stages—oral, anal, and phallic—occur during the first five years of life. Freud believed that sex-role learning is motivated by the Oedipal conflict. At approximately four years of age, the identification experience of boys and girls diverges. Resolution of the Oedipal conflict occurs by age 5, when the child identifies with the same-sex parent to receive vicariously the affection of the opposite-sex parent.[13] Emphasis is placed on the child's internal motives, the affective tie between the child and the same-sex parent (especially during the first five years of life), and the importance of sexual impulses in shaping behavior and personality development.

Cognitive development theory. Influenced by Piaget, Kohlberg theorized that sex-role development is an outgrowth of a child's cognitive organization of his social world, rather than of biological instincts or arbitrary cultural norms.[14]

Social learning theory. Social learning theorists assume that the early years of development are important, but that sex-role acquisition is a function of continuous observational learning throughout life. Such learning is based on vicarious external rewards and reinforcements from various social agents, rather than on a child's internal motives at fixed developmental stages.[15] Emphasis is placed on modeling and imitation of the dominant parent, regardless of sex and under certain conditions.

Social power framework. Parsons's "expressive-instrumental" framework views the family as part of a larger social system.[16] The father, who is the head of the family and "interpretator" to society, performs such "instrumental" role functions as decision making (an active role); the mother, in contrast, performs such "expressive" role functions as child care (a passive role). This theory stresses that the "controller of resources" is the main source of imitative behavior.

None of the theories explicates completely the predisposition of various subgroups in the population to sex-role behavior.[17] Although some theoretical tenets may have utility, it is obvious that the distinctive characteristics of minority groups and the inferior status imposed on them must be of significance in the socialization process.[18] Yet, despite basic similarities in their social position, minorities differ in the symbols that set them apart, in the nature of their relationship to the dominant group, and in their reactions to their situation.[19]

One response of profound social signficance is the dual socialization process. Although differential socialization of boys and girls generated considerable attention in the literature, the impact of race on parenting has not been a major area of inquiry until recently.[20] Dual socialization, the author believes, is a primary technique used by black families to train their children for various roles. It is a form of anticipatory socialization by which, ideally, black children acquire knowledge, skills, and impulse control that serve a dual purpose: successful mastery of a racist, hostile, and discriminatory environment and achievement of a viable social and personal "bicultural" identity.

Themes

Four recurring themes in the literature distort knowledge about black family life and yet are characteristic of the bulk of the research on black sex roles. Because of their widespread utility and suitability for demonstrating the interrelationship of various phenomena, these themes are useful here as models.

Sentimental model. This model, which Pleck termed the "boy-needs-male-model" hypothesis, assumes that if the family does not socialize its boys to masculinity, no one else does.[21] By implication, boys whose fathers are absent from the family, especially those in female-headed families, have an insecure or underdeveloped masculine identity.

Hypermasculinity model. This model assumes that boys in female-headed families are likely to develop insecure masculine identities and thus are more likely to be violent, hostile to women, or homosexual.[22]

Emasculation model. This model assumes that black men are more likely to develop insecure identities and to be emasculated because racial oppression destroys the masculinity of blacks.[23]

Matriarch model. This model assumes that black women—both those who head families and those who do not—dominate family affairs, that they exercise more power and authority and have more responsibility than their husbands or fathers relative to the cultural norms.[24]

The reader will discover that the application of these models to research on the black family has done little to advance knowledge. Rather, these models have perpetuated stereotypes, which is what research is intended not to do. In addition to the problems related to these models, another major dilemma that is pandemic to the study of black sex roles is the prevalent use of standardized normative behavioral measures that are too closely aligned with the experiences and learned skills of white middle-class people. This practice may create a systematic bias throughout the scientific process because it can obscure potential group differences. Moreover, it impedes the enhancement of a resonant seizure and appreciation of the real-life situations of black clients.

EXAMPLES OF STUDIES

Black Husband-Fathers vs. White Husband-Fathers

In an interview study, Aldous investigated the relationship between the employment status of wives and the amount of participation in the household of working-class black husband-fathers and white husband-fathers in intact families.[25] From a deficit-oriented conceptual base, she hypothesized that black husband-fathers with employed wives would be less active in performing household tasks and in decision making than would be black husband-fathers whose wives were unemployed or white husband-fathers, regardless of their wives' employment status.

ANOVA-based self-report scores of 122 white husband-fathers and 46 black husband-fathers were compared on four indexes (presumably adapted by Aldous). These four indexes were (1) the Husband's Communication Index (the extent to which the husband talked with his wife about a range of problems), (2) the Wife's Communication Index (the husband's report of his wife's communication with him), (3) the Household Task Performance Index (the extent of the husband's participation in household and child care tasks), and (4) the Decision-Making Participation Index (the husband's report of who made decisions on specific items). The range of scores on each index was 0–4, with higher scores indicating greater participation by the husband.

Aldous reported that "even with controls for family size, income and age of the youngest child, black husbands whose wives were employed performed fewer family tasks and left more family decisions to their wives. Only in the area of communication were these men slightly more active."[26] Despite this important discovery, she adversely interpreted and defined it as "problem communication." She linked it to a " 'problem-centered' conjugal relation which has given rise to or is the result of the wives' employment status."[27]

Aldous reported fewer differences among white men. Accordingly, she stated that "white men with employed wives appeared to be about as active in the home as white men whose wives were full-time homemakers."[28] She concluded: "When the wife through no choice of her own but because her husband is unemployed takes over the chief provider role, this study's findings suggest that he will abdicate his position as husband-father. And this, of course, is what the Moynihan Report argues."[29]

Clearly, Aldous's analysis was inconsistent with the data because the magnitude of the racial differences cannot be ignored. How both racial groups differed in her study was central to the tenability of the original thesis and the analysis. As Engram noted: "This is a gross distortion of the actual findings, and, as so often happens with this type of research, the researcher chooses to focus on those findings that support the thesis and either to ignore or distort the others, although these may be more convincing."[30] Such research has an "eye wash" appearance. This concept, defined by Suchman and broadened by Tripodi, refers to individuals as well as to programs.[31] It includes the possibility that the performance of individuals and programs may be undermined deliberately by attending to only those features that "look bad."

Important variables. At issue here is not whether the races differed, but how. Close inspection of Aldous's data shows that the two racial groups differed significantly on important variables of particular relevance to conjugal-role relationships. Furthermore, these differences were not fully reported.

First, specific sex-role assumptions, conceptualized in matricentric problem-oriented terms, unidirected the hypothesis to racial and sexual stereotyping. This procedure can unintentionally create systematic bias throughout the experiment. A few variable-connected confounds demonstrated that evidence supporting the hypothesis of Aldous's study was weak. For example, at the baseline, the two groups differed in important ways. White families were over-represented in the sample ($n = 122$) compared to black families ($n = 46$). The proportion of black men with full-time employed wives was 28 percent (or 13 of 46); the proportion of white men in the same category was 20 percent (or 24 of 122). Black wives as a group were more likely to be in the labor force either full time or part time (46 percent, or 21 of 46), and even more likely to have had weekly earning of less than $100, compared to white wives in this category (24 percent, or 29 of 122).

Second, in this investigation, subjects were not carefully selected or matched on background characteristics; therefore, extraneous variables, such as race, sex, and income, as well as unequal sample groups, confounded the variables being investigated. Under these circumstances, the absence of controls for these factors posed a serious threat to external validity (generalizability) because treatment effects could not be clearly evaluated. Hence, there is no way the reader can be certain that the observed differences were accounted for by the variables tested.

Significant main effects. The significant "main effects" of the study showed that

1. For these working-class men ($n = 168$), the wife's employment status was not significantly associated with the reported frequency of the husband's participation in the family with the exception of black husbands, who participated more in decision-making matters when their wives were unemployed ($p < .05$).

2. Black husband-fathers were significantly more likely to pay bills when their wives were unemployed than were white husband-fathers, although the differences were moderate.

3. Regardless of their wives' employment status, black husband-fathers were significantly more likely than were white husband-fathers to take out the garbage and twice as likely as white husband-fathers to do so when their wives were unemployed.

4. White husband-fathers were significantly more likely than were black husband-fathers to make decisions about whether their wives

Table 1.

The Participation in Marital Roles of Lower-Class Men, by Race and
Their Wives' Employment Status

	Performance of Black Men				Performance of White Men			
	Wives Employed		Wives Unemployed		Wives Employed		Wives Unemployed	
Roles	$\bar{X}$	N	$\bar{X}$	N	$\bar{X}$	N	$\bar{X}$	N
Task performance	1.5	18	1.9	28	1.4	45	1.5	77
Decision making	1.5	17	2.0	28[a]	1.8	45	1.9	76
Communication by husband	3.0	18	2.5	28	2.5	45	2.5	73
Communication by wife	3.2	18	3.0	28	2.8	45	3.0	75

SOURCE: Joan Aldous, "Wives' Employment and Lower-Class Men as Husband-Fathers: Support for the Moynihan Thesis," *Journal of Marriage and the Family*, 31 (August 1969), p. 472. Copyright © 1969 by the National Council on Family Relations, Fairview Community School Center, 1910 West County Road B, Suite 147, St. Paul, Minnesota 55113. Reprinted with permission.
[a]$F_{1, 41} = 5.69, p < .05.$

should work when their wives were unemployed, although the differences were slight. Both groups of men had parity when their wives worked and did not differ significantly.

5. Black women who worked were significantly more likely to communicate with their husbands about health problems than were white women in the same category; although the scores were significant, black women and white women who were homemakers differed slightly on this item.

6. Regardless of their wives' employment status, black husband-fathers were significantly more likely than were white husband-fathers to communicate with their wives about work problems, feelings of depression, and health problems (see Tables 1 and 2).

Significant "interaction" effects. Significant "interaction" effects showed that

1. Black husband-fathers were significantly more likely than were white husband-fathers to participate in decisions about paying bills and the amount of money to spend on clothing when their wives were unemployed.

2. When their wives were employed, white husband-fathers were

significantly more likely to participate in deciding whether to have children. Black men and white men did not differ significantly on this item when their wives were unemployed.

3. Black wives who worked were significantly more likely to communicate with their husbands about money problems than were white wives in the same category; the scores for black homemakers and white homemakers were significant, although the differences were slight on this item.

Lack of information. Furthermore, it is impossible to evaluate the results of this study without knowledge of the reliability and validity of the measures used, evidence of which was omitted. Although it is conceivable that a sound psychometric procedure was utilized, in the absence of inormation, the reader cannot draw that conclusion. It appears that Aldous was more concerned about testing Moynihan's thesis. Under these conditions, and the fact that the hypothesis under study was supported, it is difficult to determine whether the cause of the observed differences is theoretical or methodological. The absence of variance scores also impedes further meaningful interpretations of the data and may have masked real relationships. Standard deviations are useful to determine whether between-group differences are trustworthy.

The single most important point is that the results of Aldous's study should not be accepted uncritically. One essential caveat should be considered. Because they are based on faulty assumptions, non equated groups, and measures of questionable reliability and validity, the results tell us little about the nature of racial differences in family decision making and role processes. The power of ideology and the use of language, whether nonconscious or unintentional, also should not be ignored.

Child-Rearing Attitudes

Radin and Kamii measured child-rearing attitudes and class differences among forty-five "culturally disadvantaged" black mothers and fifty "middle-class" white mothers.[32] They compared the Likert-type responses of both groups and found that the black mothers and the white mothers had similar attitudes about children's rights, discipline, and welfare. The only significant difference between the two groups was that 64 percent of the black mothers but only 12 percent of the white mothers concurred with the statement, "Children should be protected from any disappointment, difficult situations, etc." Black mothers also were significantly more likely

Table 2. Performance of Lower-Class Men in Specific Marital Areas, by Race and Their Wives' Employment Status

| | Negroes | | | | Whites | | | |
| | Wives Employed | | Wives Unemployed | | Wives Employed | | Wives Unemployed | |
Roles	$\bar{X}$	N	$\bar{X}$	N	$\bar{X}$	N	$\bar{X}$	N
Task Performance								
Pays bills[a]	1.3	18	2.4	28	1.8	45	2.1	77
Takes out garbage[b]	2.9	8.0	2.8	15	1.8	24	1.4	44
Borrows money[c]	3.0	14	3.6	24	2.7	29	3.2	50
Decision Making								
Bills to pay[d]	1.7	18	2.5	27	2.2	44	1.8	73
Amount to spend on clothing[e]	1.1	18	1.9	28	1.3	44	1.2	70
Whether wife should work[f]	1.1	17	2.3	27	1.1	44	2.5	64
Whether to have children[g]	0.9	14	1.6	21	1.8	30	1.6	51
Communication by Wives								
Money problems[h]	3.7	18	3.0	25	2.9	38	3.1	62
Health problems[i]	3.5	18	3.1	27	2.8	39	3.0	70
Communication by Husbands								
Work problems[j]	2.7	16	2.5	25	2.0	41	1.9	71
Feeling depressed[k]	2.6	18	2.6	27	2.2	44	1.9	76
Health problems[l]	3.2	17	3.2	25	2.6	35	2.7	64

SOURCE: Joan Aldous, "Wives' Employment and Lower-Class Men as Husband-Fathers: Support for the Moynihan Thesis," *Journal of Marriage and the Family*, 31 (August 1969), p. 473. Copyright © 1969 by the National Council Family Relations, Fairview Community School Center, 1910 West County Road B, Suite 147, St. Paul, Minnesota 55113. Reprinted with permission.

[a] Wives' employment status, $F_{1, 164} = 6.156$, $p < .01$.
[b] Race, $F_{1, 87} = 11.294$, $p < .01$.
[c] Wives' employment status, $F_{1, 113} = 7.600$, $p < .05$.
[d] Race, by wives' employment status, $F_{1, 158} = 5.180$, $p < .05$.
[e] Race, by wives' employment status, $F_{1, 156} = 4.292$, $p < .05$.
[f] Wives' employment status, $F_{1, 147} = 22.530$, $p < .001$.
[g] Race, by wives' employment status, $F_{1, 112} = 4.143$, $p < .05$.
[h] Race, by wives' employment status, $F_{1, 139} = 4.462$, $p < .05$.
[i] Race, $F_{1, 150} = 4.126$, $p < .05$.
[j] Race, $F_{1, 149} = 6.084$, $p < .05$.
[k] Race, by wives' employment status, $F_{1, 161} = 4.518$, $p < .05$.
[l] Race, $F_{1, 137} = 5.163$, $p < .05$.

to believe that it is the mother who is ultimately responsible for the welfare of the family. In attitudes toward themselves, nuclear families, and society, black mothers tended to see themselves as suffering, having little fun, and isolated from the rest of society; they believed that they could not find consolation outside the home. However, Radin and Kamii interpreted this finding as follows: "The picture thus emerges of a suffering matriarch who confines her life to her home, deifies her own wisdom, feels no roots in society, and eyes the outside world with great suspicion."[33]

Although the verbal abilities of children were not tested, Radin and Kamii argued further that the low verbal ability of black school-age children was caused by matriarchal mothers who suppressed verbal abilities with their overwhelming authority and dominance. These overexaggerated conclusions have no empirical basis in the study. Furthermore, the comparison groups were not carefully matched. Despite the fact that almost half the black mothers headed their families compared to none of the white mothers, there is no evidence of matriarchy.

Other Matriarchy Themes

Matriarchy themes are pervasive in the literature. Plotted matriarchy scores, however, can yield divergent interpretations. Plotting, a useful technique for interpreting data, visually discriminates between groups and illustrates unequal degrees of cohesion. For example, Hyman and Reed's secondary analysis of three sample surveys of black families and white families found no significant differences between racial groups (see Table 3).[34] The authors concluded that, on average, both groups could be considered matriarchal in character.

By 1980, the form and character of the black matriarchy was alive and well. To test the "theory of status" hypothesis, Adams studied racial differences in dominant behaviors among black and white undergraduate male and female dyads.[35] This theory predicts that in initial task-oriented encounters in which there is no formal status structure, people should react to others on the basis of previously existing characteristics.[36]

Dominance was operationally defined as the number of verbal challenges against a subject's picture choice that a subject withstood each time a disagreement occurred regarding the more attractive picture of a pair. Adams found that black men were significantly more dominant only when interacting with blacks; black women were significantly more dominant than white women, black men,

Table 3.

Patterns of Male and Female Influence in Black Families and White Families (percentage)[a]

Surveys and Questions	Blacks	Whites
Gallup (1951): The most important influence when growing up was		
Father	27	31
Mother	73	69
	(68)	(1,367)
NORC (1960): The important family decisions were made by		
Father	28	23
Mother	14	13
	(93)	(858)
Decisions about disciplining children were made by		
Father	16	19
Mother	28	25
	(97)	(855)
Important family decisions by married respondents are made by		
Husband	9	6
Wife	10	7
	(67)	(628)
Decisions by married respondents with children about disciplining children are made by		
Husband	4	7
Wife	37	28
	(56)	(474)
Decisions about how the husband and wife vote are made by		
Husband	11	7
Wife	2	—
	(66)	(627)
Jennings (1965): Youths from politically divided homes who agree with		
Father	32	34
Mother	40	40
	(151)	(2,384)

[a]Reprinted by permission of the publisher from Herbert Hyman and John S. Reed, "Black Matriarchy Reconsidered: Evidence from Secondary Analysis of Sample Surveys," *Public Opinion Quarterly*, 33 (Fall 1969), pp. 346–354. Copyright © 1969 by the Trustees of Columbia University.

Table 4.

Means and Standard Deviations of Subject Groups in the Sex and Race of Subject, by Race of Confederate Interaction[a]

| | Race of Confederate | | | |
| | White | | Black | |
Subjects	*M*	*SD*	*M*	*MD*
Black men	5.74$_c$	3.68	9.08$_{a,b}$	4.02
Black women	10.31$_a$	4.12	8.73$_{a,b}$	2.95
White men	9.35$_{a,b}$	3.18	7.50$_{b,c}$	3.84
White women	6.70$_{b,c}$	2.71	6.05$_c$	6.05

SOURCE: K. A. Adams, "Who Has the Final Word? Sex, Race, and Dominant Behavior," *Journal of Personality and Social Psychology*, 38 (January 1980), p. 5. Copyright © 1980 by the American Psychological Association. Reprinted by permission of the author.

[a]Means with common subscripts do not differ significantly at the .05 level.

and white men when interacting with whites; and white men were significantly more dominant than black men when interacting with whites (see Table 4). White men and black women did not differ significantly in their interactions with blacks or whites, and the groups became more equal in dominance when interacting with a black partner. Adams concluded that white men have lost their dominant stronghold in white society and black women have retained their domineering image.

Adams's conclusions, based on the gains of women, particularly black women, and on the women's movement, seem overexaggerated. Indeed, there is no empirical evidence to substantiate the diminished dominance of white men or the escalating dominance of black women. The sample group of ninety-three volunteer psychology students of whom only thirty-two were randomly pooled from the entire student body, represents an "extreme" population group. Generalizations to other groups thus are unwarranted. Furthermore, the absence of controls for social class, race, and sex factors seriously restricts the data. Had social class been controlled for, sex and race might have had little effect on dominance.

In brief, the nature of the sampling process introduced an immediate "subject bias." Psychology students who are diverse in terms of race and sex have differential reactions to experiments.[37] As a consequence, the effect of the aforementioned factors on the rela-

tionship between sex, race, and dominant behavior is misleading
and the results have little practical import. Knowledge about the
behavior of mixed groups and interpersonal dominance might have
been advanced with careful controls.

Utility of the Research

The theoretical conceptualizations discussed in this section are inadequate to explain fully the complex pattern of behaviors that shape
black subcultures. The failure of these models to increase knowledge over time has rendered them useless for practice. Research
on black subjects requires sensitivity to cultural differences and
ethnic competence. A thorough knowledge of the dual socialization process and its connection to macro forces is fundamental to
practice. Yet, the overlap between ethnic and racial differences is
so great that decisions must rest on the study of individuals—not
of differences among groups.[38] Furthermore, despite the volume of
research, much of the evidence presented on black families has
consisted of speculative, retrospective data. Also, because researchers
have been preoccupied with absent fathers and female-headed
households, they have not studied or presented reliable information on the roles and influence of black fathers in intact families
and the emerging male-headed one-parent families.

In addition, bicultural identification (the identification with two
cultures—the black culture and the dominant culture) can lead to
role conflicts, feelings of low self-esteem and powerlessness, social
isolation, and anxiety. For example, elsewhere in this volume, Gibbs
used a multivariate technique to analyze the sources of stress,
cultural conflicts, and coping strategies of minority female graduate students.[39] She found that their conflicts were responses to
the stress of academic, family, and cultural roles; to male-female
relationships; and to career options (considered perhaps "typical"
responses to pressure by female graduate students). However, distinct
ethnic patterns emerged that are linked to and attenuated by these
students' bicultural identification.

PROPOSED INTERVENTION STRATEGIES

More and more articles and books are being published on the ethnic
factor in mental health, although the literature is still fragmented.[40]
However, much of this material has not found its way into the
curriculum of schools that train social workers and other mental

health professionals.[41] Based on this emerging literature, this section proposes a few intervention strategies to address some of the most pressing issues of black sex roles. A comprehensive understanding of black sex roles and their impact on behaviors is fundamental to effective treatment. It should enable practitioners to distinguish culture from pathology.

Work with individuals. Social workers should understand how the client defines his or her "reality" and build on the client's strengths early in treatment. Furthermore, workers should be alert to their sex-role attitudes and biases, as well as those of the client. They should use the clues that the client gives them to determine sources of latent and manifest anxieties and utilize anxiety as a motivator in treatment. Not only should social workers help clients identify the precursors to stress (such as the complexity and pressures of multiple roles), but they should assist the client in connecting these pressures to conflicts in status and roles. Once they have aided the client in identifying maladaptive responses to incompatible internal and external demands, they should help him or her to redefine the real-life situation by utilizing adaptive coping strategies (that build such skills as negotiation and conflict resolution and that encourage self-determination). Clients may need assistance in assessing role expectations, establishing role clarity, and setting realistic goals for effective role performance within time limits and personal resources. They may also need help in understanding that greater freedom means greater responsibility and risk taking. In so doing, social workers will incorporate into their intervention plans the use of key family, extended family, and community resources.

Another important task of social workers is to help clients, especially adolescents, value their femininity or masculinity in a healthy manner. They can do so by using positive male and female role models when that is warranted. Moreover, the active modeling by social workers of nonstereotypical ways that men and women can relate is central. How female and male staff members behave toward each other is more important than what they say.[42]

Work with families. Of increasing value is Solomon's empowerment paradigm for helping black families alleviate stressors caused by negative valuations and feelings of powerlessness.[43] Structural and strategic family therapy approaches also have demonstrated their utility and efficacy with a variety of symptoms, minority families, and problem groups.[44]

According to Aponte and Van Deusen, "structural family therapy is a therapeutic approach that pursues solutions to problems in their current social reality."[45] This ecostructural model "is an effort to include, along with the family, other social systems as contributors to the structure of human behavior, and to work through all these systems to achieve change."[46] In structural therapy, the focus is less on a theory of change than on a theory of family. Aponte demonstrated how family therapy with the poor and with minorities demands some fundamentally new conceptualizations about society and families and an expanded conscious use in therapy of a therapist's life experience and values.[47]

In the strategic family therapy approach, therapists take responsibility for directly influencing people by enhancing interpersonal systems to bring about beneficial change.[48] Strategic therapists "are not as concerned about family theory as they are with the theory and means for inducing change."[49]

UNFINISHED BUSINESS

At the level of policy, a few areas that will command attention in the 1980s and beyond are the enforcement of child-support payments, parent education programs for single parents (especially outreach services to single black teenage fathers reluctant to seek help, high-quality day and evening child care, continuous fund raising, good and continuous public relations, research and evaluation, greater opportunities for information feedback systems and minority researchers, and increased services to teenagers, such as Big Brothers/Big Sisters. In the area of ethnic competence, continuing education, staff development, in-service training, and consultation services are needed.[50] In relation to ethnic content, schools of social work should incorporate the contemporary literature into their curricula.

At the levels of theory and methodology, the practical assessment of blacks has been obstructed by decisive theories that have not incorporated the whole range of behaviors. Good research with representative samples and valid and reliable instrumentation is sorely needed. There is almost no limit to the amount of methodological improvement that assessment procedures need. The simple lack of norms for nonwhites on many tests makes the techniques suspect.[51] Despite the varying levels of complexity associated with solving the research problems discussed in this article, these problems inevitably must be solved. As race, sex, and ethnic factors increase in importance in the 1980s, concomitant with the stresses experienced by minorities, families will deserve the benefits of good research.

Furthermore, although the burden of proof is on the researcher, the perpetual pejorative use and abuse of data on blacks have the potential dangers of fostering exclusionary and discriminatory practices that can lead to further gatekeeping and social unrest. Professional status cannot ensure complete objectivity; however, advanced knowledge should raise practitioners above mediocrity without leading them to look down on differences. Professional avoidance of and resistance to these issues can be considered a higher form of "social irresponsibility."

Notes and References

1. Ethel H. Hall and Gloria C. King, "Working with the Strengths of Black Families," Practice Forum, *Child Welfare*, 8 (November–December 1982), p. 537.

2. Ibid.

3. Allison Davis and Robert J. Havighurst, "Social Class and Color Differences in Child Rearing," *American Sociological Review*, 11 (December 1946), pp. 698–710; Norma Radin and Constance K. Kamii, "The Child Rearing Attitudes of Disadvantaged Negro Mothers and Some Educational Implications," *Journal of Negro Education*, 34 (Spring 1965), pp. 138–146; Virginia Heyer Young, "Family and Childhood in a Southern Negro Community," *American Anthropologist*, 72 (1970), pp. 269–288; and Molly C. Dougherty, *Becoming a Woman in Rural Black Culture* (Nashville, Tenn.: Vanderbilt University Press, 1978).

4. Seymour Parker and Robert J. Kleiner, "Characteristics of Negro Mothers in Single-Headed Households," *Journal of Marriage and the Family*, 28 (November 1966), pp. 507–513; Marie Peters and Cecile de Ford, "The Solo Mother," in Robert Staples, ed., *The Black Family: Essays and Studies* (2d ed.; Belmont, Calif.: Wadsworth Publishing Co., 1978), pp. 192–199; Prudence Brown, Lorraine Perry, and Ernest Hamburg, "Sex-Role Attitudes and Psychological Outcomes for Black and White Women Experiencing Marital Dissolution," *Journal of Marriage and the Family*, 39 (August 1977), pp. 549–561; and C. Ailen Haney et al., "Characteristics of Black Women in Male and Female Households," *Journal of Black Studies*, 6 (December 1975), pp. 136–157.

5. Marjorie Random Hershey, "Racial Differences in Sex-Role Identities and Sex Stereotyping: Evidence Against a Common Assumption," *Social Science Quarterly*, 58 (March 1978), pp. 583–596; and John Scanzoni, "Sex Roles, Economic Factors, and Marital Solidarity in Black and White Marriages," *Journal of Marriage and the Family*, 36 (February 1975), pp. 130–144.

6. For a well-documented critical analysis, see Elizabeth Herzog and Cecilia Sudia, "Children in Fatherless Families," in Bettye M. Caldwell and Henry N. Ricciuti, eds., *Review of Child Development Research*, Vol. 3 (Chicago: University of Chicago Press, 1973); and Heather L. Ross and Isabel V. Sawhill, "Race and Family Structures: Differences in Marital Stability," *In Time of Transition* (Washington, D.C.: The Urban Institute, 1975), pp. 129–157.

7. For a broad synthesis of research on black families, see Eleanor Engram, *Science, Myth, Reality: The Black Family in One Half Century of Research* (Westport, Conn.: Greenwood Press, 1982).

8. John Scanzoni and Greer Litton-Fox, "Sex Roles, Family and Society: The Seventies and Beyond," *Journal of Marriage and the Family*, 42 (November 1980), p. 752.

9. R. Linton, "Age and Sex Categories," *American Sociological Review*, 7 (1936), pp. 589–693.

10. Patrick C. Lee and Robert S. Stewart, *Sex Differences: Cultural and Developmental Dimensions* (New York: Urizen Books, 1976).

11. Jeanne H. Block, "Conceptions of Sex-Role: Some Cross-Cultural Perspectives," *American Psychologist*, 28 (1973), pp. 512–526.

12. John Scanzoni, *The Black Family in Modern Society* (Boston: Allyn & Bacon, 1971), p. 19.

13. See Sigmund Freud, *New Introductory Lectures in Psychoanalysis*, James Strachey, ed. and trans. (New York: W. W. Norton & Co., 1965); Freud, "Some Psychological Consequences of the Anatomical Distinction Between the Sexes," *Collected Papers of Sigmund Freud*, Vol. 5 (London, England: Hogarth Press, 1950), pp. 186–197; Freud, "The Passing of the Oedipus Complex," *Collected Papers of Sigmund Freud*, Vol. 2 (London, England: Hogarth Press, 1924); and Freud, "The Dissolution of the Oedipus Complex," *Complete Psychological Works of Sigmund Freud*, Vol. 19 (London, England: Hogarth Press, 1961), pp. 173–179.

14. Jean Piaget, *The Origins of Intelligence* (New York: International Universities Press, 1952); Piaget, *The Child's Construction of Reality* (New York: Basic Books, 1954); and L. Kohlberg, "A Cognitive-Developmental Analysis of Children's Sex-Role Concepts and Attitudes," in Eleanor E. Maccoby, ed., *The Development of Sex Differences* (Stanford, Calif.: Stanford University Press, 1966).

15. See Albert Bandura, *Social Learning Theory* (Englewood Cliffs, N.J.: Prentice-Hall, 1977); Bandura, "Social-Learning Theory of Identificatory Processes," in David A. Goslin, ed., *Handbook of Socialization Theory and Research* (Chicago: Rand McNally & Co., 1969), pp. 213–262; Bandura, D. Ross, and S. A. Ross, "Vicarious Reinforcement and Imitative Learning," *Journal of Abnormal and Social Psychology*, 67 (1963), pp. 601–607; Bandura and Richard H. Walters, *Social Learning and Personality* (New York: Holt, Rinehart & Winston, 1963); and Walter Mischel, "Sex-Typing and Socialization," in Paul H. Mussen, ed., *Carmichael's Manual of Child Psychology* (3d ed.; New York: John Wiley & Sons, 1970), pp. 3–72.

16. Talcott Parsons, "Family Structure and Socialization of the Child," in Parsons and Robert F. Bales, eds., *Family, Socialization and Interaction Process* (Glencoe, Ill.: Free Press, 1955), pp. 35–131.

17. See Irene H. Frieze, *Women and Sex Roles: Social Psychological Perspective* (New York: W. W. Norton & Co., 1978), p. 133.

18. Donald R. Young, "The Socialization of American Minority Peoples," in David A. Goslin, ed., *Handbook of Socialization Theory and Research* (Chicago: Rand McNally Co., 1969), pp. 1103–1140.

19. George E. Simpson and J. Milton Yinger, *Racial and Cultural Minorities: An Analysis of Prejudice and Discrimination* (4th ed.; New York: Harper & Row, 1972).

20. Marie F. Peters, "Parenting in Black Families with Young Children: A Historical Perspective," in Harriette P. McAdoo, ed., *Black Families* (Beverly Hills, Calif.: Sage Publications, 1981), pp. 213–224.

21. Joseph H. Pleck, "Prisoners of Manliness," *Psychology Today*, 15 (September 1981), p. 72. See also Doris Wildinson and Ronald L. Taylor, eds., *The Black Male in America* (Chicago: Nelson-Hall, 1977), p. 43.

22. Pleck, "Prisoners of Manliness," pp. 74–75.

23. Ibid., p. 79.

24. Ross and Sawhill, "Race and Family Structures."

25. Joan Aldous, "Wives' Employment and Lower-Class Men as Husband-Fathers: Support for the Moynihan Thesis," *Journal of Marriage and the Family*, 31 (August 1969), pp. 469–476.

26. Ibid., p. 472.

27. Ibid., p. 475.

28. Ibid., p. 472.

29. Ibid., p. 476.

30. See Engram, *Science, Myth, Reality*, p. 70.

31. Edward A. Suchman, *Evaluative Research* (New York: Russell Sage Foundation, 1967), p. 143; and Tony Tripodi, *Uses and Abuses of Social Research in Social Work* (New York: Columbia University Press, 1974), esp. note 29, p. 215.

32. Radin and Kamii, "The Child Rearing Attitudes of Disadvantaged Negro Mothers and Some Educational Implications."

33. Ibid., p. 142.

34. Herbert Hyman and John S. Reed, "Black Matriarchy Reconsidered: Evidence from Secondary Analysis of Sample Surveys," *Public Opinion Quarterly*, 33 (Fall 1969), pp. 346–354.

35. Kathryn A. Adams, "Who Has the Final Word? Sex, Race, and Dominant Behavior," *Journal of Personality and Social Psychology*, 38 (January 1980), pp. 1–8.

36. For a discussion of the theory of status, see Joseph Berger, Bernard P. Cohen, and Morris Zelditch, "Status Characteristics and Social Interaction," *American Sociological Review*, 37 (1972), pp. 241–255; and D. W. Carment, "Effect of Sex-Role in Maximizing Differences Game," *Journal of Conflict Resolution*, 18 (1974), pp. 461–472.

37. John P. Dolly et al., "The Influence of Sex and Race on the Test Scores of Research Subjects Exposed to Research Purpose Information," *Journal of Psychology*, 103 (June 1979), pp. 61–65.

38. Norman D. Sundberg, *Assessment of Persons* (Englewood Cliffs, N.J.: Prentice-Hall, 1977), p. 290.

39. Jewelle Taylor Gibbs, "Conflicts and Coping Strategies of Minority Female Graduate Students," this volume, pp 22–36.

40. See, for example, Joseph Giordano and Grace P. Giordano, *The Ethno-Cultural Factor in Mental Health: A Literature Review and Bibliography* (New York: Institute on Pluralism and Group Identity of the American Jewish Committee, 1977); Monica McGoldrick, John K. Pearce, and Giordano, eds., *Ethnicity and Family Therapy* (New York: Guilford Press, 1982); Harry J. Aponte and J. M. Van Deusen, "Structural Family Therapy," in Alan S. Gurman and David P. Kniskern, eds., *Handbook of Family Therapy* (New York: Brunner/Mazel, 1981), pp. 310–360; Armando Morales, "Social Work with Third-World People," *Social Work*, 26 (January 1981), pp. 45–51; Wynetta Devore and Elfriede Schlesinger, *Ethnic-Sensitive Social Work Practice* (St. Louis, Mo.: C. V. Mosby Co., 1981); Doman Lum, "Toward a Framework for Social Work Practice with Minorities," *Social Work*, 27 (May 1982), pp. 244–249; James W. Green, *Cultural Awareness in the Human Services* (Englewood Cliffs, N.J.: Prentice-Hall, 1982); Hall and King, "Working with the Strengths of Black Families"; J. W. Leigh and James W. Green, "The Structure of the Black Community: The Knowledge Base for Social Services," in Green, ed., *Cultural Awareness in the Human Services*, pp. 94–121;

Shirley Jenkins, *The Ethnic Dilemma in Social Services* (New York: Free Press, 1981); and "Social Work and People of Color," *Social Work*, 27 (January 1982), entire issue.

41. Giordano and Giordano, *The Ethno-Cultural Factor in Mental Health.*

42. Beth Reed and Rebecca Moise, "Implications for Treatment and Future Research," *Addicted Women: Family Dynamics, Self-Perceptions, and Support Systems*, National Institute on Drug Abuse Monograph Series (Washington, D.C.: U.S. Government Printing Office, 1979), pp. 114–130; and Gibbs, "Conflicts and Coping Strategies of Minority Female Graduate Students."

43. Barbara Solomon, *Black Empowerment* (New York: Columbia University Press, 1976).

44. See Aponte and Van Deusen, "Structural Family Therapy"; Salvador Minuchin et al., *Families of the Slums* (New York: Basic Books, 1967); M. Duncan Stanton, "Marital Therapy from a Structural/Stratègic Viewpoint," in G. P. Sholevar, ed., *Handbook of Family Therapy* (New York: Brunner/Mazel, 1981); and Stanton et al., *The Family Therapy of Drug Abuse and Addiction* (New York: Guilford Press, 1982).

45. Aponte and Van Deusen, "Structural Family Therapy," p. 338.

46. Ibid., p. 311.

47. Harry J. Aponte, "Family Therapy with Minority Families." Paper presented at the preconference institute, NASW Minority Issues Conference: Color in a White Society," Los Angeles, Calif., June 1982.

48. Jay Haley, *Uncommon Therapy* (New York: W. W. Norton & Co., 1973).

49. Stanton et al., *The Family Therapy of Drug Abuse and Addiction*, p. 115.

50. Joseph S. Gallegos, "The Ethnic Competence Model for Social Work Education," this volume, pp. 1–9.

51. Sundberg, *Assessment of Persons*, p. 290.

Black Men in White America: Critical Issues

Lawrence E. Gary and Bogart R. Leashore

Social scientists and social service providers have generally viewed the black man from a negative perspective. Not only have they attributed problems in family stability and child development to his absence, but they have either ignored him or used coercive approaches with him in service delivery.[1] In short, both researchers and practitioners have failed to view the black man as a major resource person for the black family and black children. Much of this failure is rooted in racism and discrimination that produced the long-standing but incorrect myths and stereotypes which depict the black man as irresponsible, ineffective, and frequently invisible and represent him as a street-corner man, pimp, deserter, criminal, or hustler. The mass media, especially television, continue to reinforce these images.

Few systematic attempts have been made to explore, analyze, and document the life circumstances of black men in white America. Only in the last decade have social workers, sociologists, and others begun to produce works based on nonpathological models and non-captive and diverse groups of black men.[2] In line with this emerging trend, the authors address some critical issues facing black men by examining social, economic, and health indicators for black men from several national sources of data and comparing these indicators to those for white men. In addition, they analyze the data from an exploratory study of black men in a large metropolitan area and present implications for social work intervention on these critical issues.

The theoretical framework used to identify and analyze the critical

115

issues, as well as the implications for social work intervention, is that institutional racism accounts for the inequities experienced by black men. "Institutional racism" is defined as "that complex of institutional arrangements that restrict the life choices of black Americans in comparison to those of white Americans;...the restrictive consequence is the important fact rather than formal intention."[3] Although black men may enjoy certain privileges because of institutional sexism, the critical issues discussed in this article are largely the result of institutional racism. As Staples observed, the racial subordination of black men "has more than cancelled out their advantages as males in the larger society."[4]

SOCIAL, ECONOMIC, AND HEALTH INDICATORS

A composite view of the life circumstances of black men can be ascertained by examining important social, economic, and health indicators, such as education, income, unemployment, life expectancy, and death rates. These indicators point to distinct differences between black men and white men. For example, the median number of years of school completed by black men in 1978 was 11.6 years, compared to 12.6 years for white men. The median annual family income for male-headed black families in 1977 was $13,443, compared to $17,848 for male-headed white families. In addition, the unemployment rate for black men, aged 20 and older, was nearly three times that of white men in 1979 (9.1 and 3.6, respectively). Among employed men in 1977, nearly twice as many white men as black men were white-collar workers, while more than twice as many black men as white men were service workers. In the same year, 58 percent of black men were blue-collar workers, compared to 42 percent of white men.

An examination of criminal-victimization rates for 1977 indicates that 57.4 percent of black men but only 45.3 percent of white men, aged 12 and older, were victims of crime. In the same year, the life expectancy rate at birth of nonwhite men (90 percent of whom were black) was considerably shorter than that of white men (64.6 years versus 70 years). Similarly, the age-adjusted death rate was higher for black men (1,127.6) than for white men (781.5) per 100,000 population. In 1975, the age-adjusted admission rates for outpatient and inpatient psychiatric services were higher for black men than for white men. Specifically, 729.7 black men, compared to 587.7 white men per 100,000 population, were admitted to state and county mental hospitals for outpatient psychiatric services, while

Table 1.

Social, Economic, and Health Profile of Black Men

Indicators (Selected Years)	Black Men	White Men
Number of males to 100 females, 1978	90.6	95.3
Median school years completed, 1978	11.6	12.6
Median family income of male-headed families, 1977	$13,443	$17,848
Unemployment rates for civilians, aged 20 years and older, 1979	9.1[a]	3.6
Unemployment rates of male Vietnam-era veterans, 20–24 years old, 1979	20.5[a]	9.8
Percentage of employed white-collar workers, 1977	23.0	42.0
Percentage of employed blue-collar workers, 1977	58.0	45.0
Percentage of employed service workers, 1977	17.0	8.0
Victimization rates per 1,000 for persons aged 12 and older, crimes of violence, 1977	57.4	45.3
Life expectancy at birth, 1977	54.6	70.0
Age-adjusted death rates per 100,000, 1977	1,127.6	781.5
Age-adjusted admission rates per 100,000 for outpatient psychiatric services, 1975	729.7	587.7
Age-adjusted admission rates per 100,000 for inpatient state and county psychiatric services, 1975	509.8	213.2

SOURCES: U.S. Bureau of the Census, *Statistical Abstract of the United States: 1979* (Washington, D.C.: U.S. Government Printing Office, 1979), pp. 28–29, 70, and 79; U.S. Bureau of the Census, *The Social and Economic Status of the Black Population in the United States: 1970–1978* (Washington, D.C.: U.S. Government Printing Office, 1979), pp. 109, 174, 190, and 218; U.S. Department of Labor, *Employment and Training Report of the President* (Washington, D.C.: U.S. Government Printing Office, 1980), pp. 225–226, 230, 231–234, and 254; U.S. Department of Justice, *Criminal Victimization in the United States* (Washington, D.C.: U.S. Government Printing Office, 1979), p. 24; and Office of Health Resources Opportunity, *Health of the Disadvantaged: Chartbook III* (Washington, D.C.: U.S. Government Printing Office, 1980), pp. 86, 89.

[a]These data include blacks and other racial groups. Blacks represent about 90 percent of those classified as "black and others."

509.8 black men and 213.2 white men per 100,000 population were admitted for inpatient psychiatric services. These, as well as other indicators, are presented in Table 1.

Limited educational opportunities and attainment invariably lead to restricted employment and income, which, in turn, make it difficult to meet one's needs, as well as those of one's family. For many black men, the inability to support their families is a source of ongoing frustration. Although some black men manage to cope and adapt within the sanctions of society, others turn to illegal activities. For too many black men, illegal activities result in incarceration and ultimately in separation from their families. The short life expectancy, high death rate, and high psychiatric institutionalization rate of black men also have a significant effect on the lives of black families.[5]

DAY-TO-DAY CONCERNS OF BLACK MEN

Few attempts have been made to determine how black men perceive and experience their day-to-day concerns. For the most part, those studies that have been done involved small samples of low-income black men.[6] Recognizing the limitations of these studies and the need for additional research, the Mental Health Research and Development Center at Howard University undertook a study of adult black men in 1978. One hundred forty-two black men, aged 18–65, who resided in the metropolitan Washington, D.C., area were interviewed regarding their day-to-day concerns and problems, as well as their sources of help. As a nonprobability sample, the men were recruited through computer-generated random telephone numbers, from barber shops frequented by black men, and through individual referrals.[7]

A sociodemographic profile of the sample is presented in Table 2, which includes comparative data for black men in the District of Columbia and its Standard Metropolitan Statistical Area (SMSA) obtained from the 1970 census.[8] As can be seen, a larger percentage of men in the sample (79 percent) were under 45 years than were those in the District of Columbia (61 percent) and in its SMSA (64 percent). Further, the percentages of married men in the District of Columbia (60 percent) and its SMSA (62 percent) were nearly twice as high as that of the sample (33 percent). Conversely, the percentage of never-married men in the sample (46 percent) was nearly twice as high as those for the District of Columbia (25 percent) and its SMSA (23 percent). Although comparable percentages of the men in the study (26 percent) and in the District of Columbia (29 percent) and its SMSA (29 percent) had twelve years of education, the percentage of men in the study (51 percent) with more than twelve years of education was more than three times the percentages for the District of Columbia (15 percent) and its SMSA (16 percent). In comparison with the District of Columbia and its SMSA, the study sample consisted of a smaller percentage of men with low family incomes and a corresponding larger percen-

Table 2.

Demographic Characteristics of the Sample and of the Black Male Population of Washington, D.C., and Its Standard Metropolitan Statistical Area (SMSA), Based on Data from the 1970 Census[a]

	Sample		1970 Census Data	
Characteristic	Number	Percentage	Washington, D.C. (percentage)	SMSA (percentage)
Age				
18–24 years	23	16	16	17
25–34 years	64	45	25	26
35–44 years	25	18	20	21
45–54 years	19	13	18	16
55 years and over	11	8	21	18
Total	142	100	100	100
Marital Status				
Married	46	33	60	62
Never married	64	46	25	23
Separated	12	9	8	8
Divorced	17	12	4	3
Total	139[b]	100	97[c]	96[d]
Education				
Less than 12 years	33	23	56	55
12 years	36	26	29	29
More than 12 years	73	51	15	16
Total	142	100	100	100
Family Income				
Less than $6,000	20	16	31	30
$6,000–9,999	29	22	28	28
$10,000–14,999	20	16	24	24
$15,000–24,999	37	28	14	15
$25,000 and above	23	18	3	3
Total	129[e]	100	100	100
Employment Status				
Employed	91	77	76	76
Unemployed	30	3	3	3
Not in labor force	18[f]	20	21	21
Total	139[g]	100	100	100

SOURCE: U.S. Department of Commerce, *1970 Census of the Population, Characteristics of the Population* (Washington, D.C.: U.S. Government Printing Office, 1972), Vol. 1, Part 10.

[a] Data are rounded; 1970 census data are for black men, aged 18+ years.
[b] Data are missing for three men, one of whom was a widower.
[c] Excludes 3 percent who were widowed.
[d] Excludes 4 percent who were widowed.
[e] Data are missing for thirteen men.
[f] Includes full-time students and retired and disabled persons.
[g] Data are missing for three men.

tage of men with middle and upper family incomes. Employment status was comparable for the men in the study and those enumerated by the census.[9]

Exploration of the day-to-day concerns and problems of the men in the study involved a series of open- and closed-ended questions. Concerns and problems were classified into four types: (1) personal, (2) interpersonal, (3) economic, and (4) social. Personal problems focused on the individual; that is, problems that did not appear to involve others directly and which seemed to require major efforts on the individual's part for resolution. These problems were of a physical or psychological nature, such as health problems, problems with alcohol or drugs, and psychological difficulties, including fear, despair, and depression. Interpersonal problems were those that seemed to emphasize the individual and his relationship with those in his immediate and informal environment, that is, family and friends. Relationships were distinguished by their informal and personal quality and included relationships with a spouse or mate, parents, children, friends, and peers. Economic problems were those that specifically involved economic or work-related concerns, such as inadequate income, economic survival, unemployment, and underemployment. Social problems were those that involved such areas as human services, education, and civil rights or liberties, including racism and discrimination, lack of education, and harrassment by the police. The designation of problems in the four categories was not always clear. However, because the purpose of the classification was descriptive, it was not developed to address definitively the nature or the source of problems faced by the men.

Each respondent was asked an open-ended question regarding his perception of the most serious problems confronting black men as a group. The most frequently mentioned type of problem was economic (45 percent), which was followed by social (32 percent), personal (16 percent), and interpersonal (7 percent). When these problems were analyzed for within-group differences according to age, marital and work status, family income, and education, only work status was statistically significant; that is, more than half the employed men perceived economic problems as the most serious problem confronting black men, while almost one-third of the unemployed men reported social problems as the most serious.

When questioned about which was the "biggest problem" they had experienced personally during their lives, 31 percent mentioned economic problems; 26 percent, personal problems; 22 percent, social problems; and 21 percent, interpersonal problems. When the responses of the married and unmarried men were examined with respect to these problems, the distributions differed at the .05 level (X^2 = .0267, df = 1); the married men most frequently reported economic difficulties, and the unmarried men most frequently reported interpersonal problems. Interpersonal problems were most frequently mentioned by men with annual family incomes of less than $8,000, while men with annual family incomes of $8,000 or more most frequently reported economic problems as their "biggest" lifetime problem. The distributions were statistically significant at the .05 level (X^2 = .0246, df = 1). No significant differences were found when the "biggest" lifetime problems were examined by age, work status, and education.

HELP-SEEKING BEHAVIOR OF BLACK MEN

The men in the study were asked several questions about their comfort and ease in seeking help, the frequency of their seeking help, their ability to get help when needed, and their preferred helping resources. For the purposes of the study, "help seeking" was defined as requesting advice and material assistance—actions aimed at problem solving. Eighty percent of the men said they preferred to solve their own problems, and 20 percent stated they tended to ask others for advice. However, when queried further as to their feelings about asking others for help when they actually needed it, the responses were almost evenly distributed; 35 percent reported they did not mind asking others for help when needed, followed by 34 percent who mildly disliked doing so, and 31 percent who strongly disliked it.

With regard to the frequency of asking for advice, 40 percent of the men indicated they almost never asked for advice, 38 percent said they would sometimes ask for advice, and 14 percent reported they would frequently ask for advice. The majority thought they were either very good (52 percent) or about average (35 percent) at persuading others to help them; only 13 percent rated themselves as being below average at acquiring aid from others.

As a follow-up to the question about their "biggest" lifetime problem, the men were asked what they had done about the problem. They were classified either as help seekers or nonseekers on the basis of their responses. Those in the help seeker category had made such statements as "sought professional help," "asked parents for aid or advice," or "filed for a divorce." Those who said they "just prayed," "accepted reality," and "tried to understand myself" were included in the nonseeker category. This procedure revealed an even distribution of men ($n = 130$) who were help seekers (50 percent) or nonseekers (50 percent). Demographic variables such as age ($\chi^2 = 1.6$, $df = 1$), education ($\chi^2 = 0.0$, $df = 1$), marital status ($\chi^2 = .10$, $df = 1$), employment status ($\chi^2 = 1.3$, $df = 1$), and family income ($\chi^2 = 1.4$, $df = 1$) were not significant in distinguishing help seekers from nonseekers.

To explore further their orientation to help seeking, the men were asked the following open-ended question: "If you had a serious emotional problem, such as being very depressed, very nervous, or very anxious, where would you go for help?" Their responses were subsequently categorized as formal, informal, or self-reliant. Of the 137 men who responded, 44 percent preferred an informal source of assistance (friends, wife, or family), and 42 percent were more inclined to use a formal source (a hospital, physician, psychiatrist, or community mental health center); 14 percent indicated a preference for self-reliance.

When asked about the person they "really opened up to the most over the past year," 16 of the 140 men reported they had not opened up to anyone. However, of the 124 men who had done so, 56 percent most frequently mentioned a family member, 40 percent mentioned a friend, and the remaining 4 percent reported other sources. A wife or mother was the most frequently mentioned family member, and a girlfriend was the most often mentioned friend.

IMPLICATIONS FOR SOCIAL WORK

The national indicators and the findings from the exploratory study of black men clearly demonstrate that economic factors have a major impact on the lives of black men. Therefore, if social work practice is to be effective with black men, issues of unemployment, inadequate income, inadequate health care, racism, and discrimination cannot be ignored. Contemporary service delivery systems will have to go beyond individual pathology to address the economic oppression of black men, as well as others, in several arenas— employment, criminal justice, and health care. The achievement of full employment, an adequate guaranteed income, and an adequate program of national health insurance are three social welfare goals that can make significant and positive changes in the lives of black men and all Americans. Social work should strengthen its efforts to achieve these goals both within the profession and through coalition building and social action.

Other institutional changes are needed to address the inequities endured by black men. For example, the short life expectancy of black men precludes many from receiving social security benefits. Thus, consideration should be given to changing the age requirements for receiving benefits so that life expectancy rates of various subgroups are taken into account. Black men and others with a shorter life expectancy may thus become eligible for benefits earlier than those with a longer life expectancy. Furthermore, black men should be given greater opportunities to benefit from programs involving alternatives to incarceration, such as restitution, pretrial intervention, and weekend incarceration.

Social workers and others can help prevent the institutionalization of black men in correctional and psychiatric facilities by providing meaningful services. However, before social workers can do so, they must strive to eliminate individual and institutional racism. They can eliminate individual racism by examining their attitudes and beliefs about their behavior toward black people in general and black men in particular. Agencies, organizations, and professionals can work to end institutional racism by identifying and eliminating racist attitudes, practices, and policies that impinge on their ability to render effective services to black men. Stereotypes, misconceptions, inaccessible services, ineffective service approaches, staffing, and specific policies may communicate to black men that they should avoid contact with such agencies and organizations.

Failure to recognize and appreciate the value system of black people can be a major obstacle to effective service delivery. For example, kinship ties and mutual support have been significant factors in the ability of many black families to survive and remain stable.[10] It is indeed the skilled practitioner who can identify, assess, and use kinship ties and significant others in the interest of his or her client. Moreover, in providing direct services to black men, clinging to restrictive therapeutic approaches can seriously impede the development of a trusting, honest, and helping relationship. In those cases in which there is no "visible" black man (such as in female-headed households), an assessment of kinship and other informal ties may reveal not only the active involvement of a black man or men, but the presence of a black man who can contribute to the helping process. Brothers, uncles, grandfathers, neighbors, fictive kin, and even the "man down the street" often serve as significant persons in the lives of black clients. They should not be overlooked.

In addition to changes in social welfare policies and institutional and individual practices, the black community in general should utilize and build its resources in behalf of all black people, including black men. Following its tradition of mutual aid, the black church should expand its family activities by making special efforts to involve black men. Churches and social and civic organizations should establish job banks and provide special loan funds and shelter for individuals and families in crisis situations. Black institutions and organizations should form credit unions and investment corporations to promote the economic and general well-being of black men and their families. Groups and organizations of black men should be formed to provide mutual support and services to black people, such as educational and vocational programs for institutionalized black men. Finally, black men and black people in general should actively engage in the political arena through voter education programs and by offering their support to political candidates who will act in the best interests of black people.

Notes and References

1. See R. V. Burton and J. M. Whitting, "The Absent Father and Cross Sex Identity," *Merrill-Palmer Quarterly*, 7 (July 1961), pp. 85–95; E. Mavis Hetherington, "Effects of Paternal Absence on Sex-typed Behaviors in Negro and White Males," *Journal of Personality and Social Psychology*, 4 (July 1966), pp. 87–91; R. H. Rubin, "Adult Males and the Self Attitudes of Black Children," *Child Study Journal*, 4 (1974), pp. 33–36; Marybeth Shinn, "Father Absence and Children's Cognitive Development," *Psychological Bulletin*, 85 (March 1978), pp. 295–324; Bogart R. Leashore, "Social Services and Black Men," in Lawrence E. Gary, ed., *Black Men* (Beverly Hills: Sage Publications, 1981), pp. 257–267.

2. See Lawrence E. Gary et al., *Help-Seeking Behavior Among Black Men* (Washington, D.C.: Institute for Urban Affairs and Research, Howard University, 1982); Robert Staples, "Masculinity and Race: The Dual Dilemma of Black Men," *Journal of Social Issues*, 34 (Winter 1978), pp. 169–170; Gary, ed., *Black Men*; D. Wilkinson and R. Traylor, *The Black Male in America* (Chicago: Nelson-Hall, 1977); Gary and Bogart R. Leashore, "High-risk Status of Black Men," *Social Work*, 27 (January 1982), pp. 54–58; Thomas J. Hopkins, "The Role of the Agency in Supporting Black Manhood," *Social Work*, 18 (January 1973), pp. 53–58; Samuel Tuck, Jr., "A Mode for Working with Black Fathers, *American Journal of Orthopsychiatry*, 41 (April 1971), pp. 465–472; and Noel A. Cazenave, "Middle-Income Black Fathers: An Analysis of Provider Roles," *Family Coordinator*, 28 (October 1979), pp. 583–592.

3. See Thomas F. Pettigrew, "Racism and Mental Health of White Americans," in Charles Willie, Bernard M. Kramer, and Bertram Brown, eds., *Racism and Mental Health* (Pittsburgh: University of Pittsburgh Press, 1971), pp. 274–275.

4. See Staples, "Masculinity and Race."

5. For a fuller explication of these indicators, see Gary and Leashore, "High-risk Status of Black Men."

6. See Elliott Liebow, *Tally's Corner* (Boston: Little, Brown & Co., 1967); and Aaron L. Rutledge and Gertrude Z. Gass, *Nineteen Negro Men* (San Francisco: Jossey-Bass, 1967).

7. Gary et al., *Help-Seeking Behavior Among Black Men.*

8. This study was conducted before the 1980 census was undertaken.

9. Gary et al., *Help-Seeking Behavior Among Black Men.*

10. Robert Hill, *Strengths of Black Families* (Washington, D.C.: National Urban League, 1971); W. Hays and C. Mindel, "Extended Kinship Relations in Black and White Families," *Journal of Marriage and the Family*, 35 (February 1973), pp. 51–57; Andrew Billingsley, *Black Families in White America* (Englewood Cliffs, N.J.: Prentice-Hall, 1968); Harriette P. McAdoo, "Factors Related to Stability in Upwardly Mobile Black Families," *Journal of Marriage and the Family*, 40 (November 1978), pp. 761–776; Lena Wright Myers, *Black Women: Do They Cope Better?* (Englewood Cliffs, N.J.: Prentice-Hall, 1980); and Carol Stack, *All Our Kin* (New York: Harper & Row, 1974).

Role of the Black Community in Reducing Infant Mortality

Carol Hill Lowe

In the United States today, black babies are dying at a rate which is twice that of white babies and those of other minority groups.[1] In the District of Columbia—a "city-state" with an urban population that is 72 percent black—the risk of death for black infants is almost three times higher than that for white infants.[2] (Washington, D.C., has had the notoriety of having more babies die before one year of age than comparable cities with populations of 500,000.) The disparity between the mortality rates of white infants and black infants is a public health and political issue, both locally and nationally.

Low birth weight is the single most significant factor associated with the death of infants.[3] Moreover, the difference in mortality rates for black babies and for white babies in the District of Columbia and in the nation as a whole is directly related to the higher incidence of low birth weight (1,500 grams and under) among black infants.[4] That the high death rate of black infants is directly related to their low birth weight indicates the need to consider broad socioeconomic factors in defining and implementing strategies to reduce infant mortality in a minority population.

COMPLEX INDICATORS

Race has traditionally been considered an important public health indicator of infant mortality. Pregnant black women in the District of Columbia who are poor, undereducated, and unmarried (over 60 percent) and lack preventive and prenatal care have twice the

126

number of low birth-weight babies as do other women.[5] However, Boone's in-depth study of this population suggests that there are other nontraditional indicators—besides class, marital status, age, and education—that single out disadvantaged black women as being at the highest risk of a poor pregnancy outcome.[6] The study found that these women generally are underweight, abuse nicotine and alcohol, use contraceptives ineffectively, are migrants from a southern state, experience frequent and unsuccessful pregnancies, are generally in poor health, tend to be psychologically depressed because of poor primary relationships and the lack of support systems, and are victims of emotional and physical abuse. Economic factors, correlated with educational attainment, age, the number of pregnancies, prepregnancy weight and dietary habits, smoking and alcohol consumption, the utilization of prenatal and family planning services, and a family history of mental retardation and early childbearing highlight some of the differences between minority and non-minority women. Race, as an indicator of high-risk conditions, therefore, is primarily a correlation with other socioeconomic and medical variables, rather than a unique or isolated determinant.

The element of race has to be viewed also in the context of differences in the utilization of the health care delivery system by various ethnic and cultural groups and of the priority that an economically disadvantaged group places on health and the prevention of illness. Furthermore, the health care system tends to respond to patients who use the system rather than to reach out to groups that do not.

Historically, the professional health community has been divided socioeconomically into private medical providers and public medical providers, each addressing the needs of its constituency. Local governments did not encourage them to work together on shared problems. Although most health care services have been provided by the private sector, health care for the poor has been provided primarily by public health departments.

Because of the array of health care providers and facilities in Washington, D.C., it has long been recognized that cooperative planning, organization, and delivery of regionalized health care services are necessary if pregnancy outcomes are to be improved. However, there has been some debate over the best way to reduce the number of dying babies. There have been arguments over preventive intervention versus curative intervention, over the futility of trying to save low birth-weight babies, and over separating the infant mortality issue from efforts to curb teenage pregnancies.

IMPROVED PREGNANCY OUTCOME PROJECTS

In 1977, the U.S. Department of Health and Human Services established and funded the Improved Pregnancy Outcome Projects (IPOs). This action reflected the federal government's intent to blend prevention, direct services, and advocacy approaches to provide optimal health care services to mothers and children. Five years long, the individual IPO projects were deliberately placed in jurisdictions that had high rates of infant mortality and of births to teenagers, as well as the greatest shortages in health care manpower. Washington, D.C., was selected as one site.

The specific objectives of the grants were as follows:

1. To promote preventive services.
2. To coordinate all programs offering maternity and infant care services in IPO states.
3. To improve maternity care.
4. To reduce mortality and morbidity associated with childbearing and infancy.
5. To promote regionalized perinatal care.

The basis for these objectives was the premise that a combination of early prenatal care, family planning, nutrition, health education, and the provision of social services improves the chances for a positive pregnancy outcome. The IPO projects were encouraged to build strategies based on this premise.[7]

STRATEGIES

Because the subgoals for the reduction of infant mortality are broad and the issue is highly politicized, the IPO in Washington, D.C., created strategies to address these two concerns as well as the basic goal of prevention. Short-term programs were developed to satisfy those in the medical community who were obsessed with the controversial "doctrine of specific etiology," which emphasizes a strictly medical cause of the problem. Then, interventions were developed, based on the recognition that the configuration of health services and resources in an area are a *system*—a collection of interrelated components that collectively affect the health status and well-being of the population.

The interest in and commitment of social work to community organization meant that emphasis was placed on a multifactorial analysis of the problem, including knowledge and use of measures and institutions that influence the care of mothers and children.

This primary prevention model, integrated with social change theory, involved a combination of social work skills and perspectives, the public health philosophy of prevention, and, most important, a deep respect for and valuing of the importance of the community's addressing its needs and in defining its activities.[8]

Because black people have such a high proportion of maternity-related and other reproductive health problems, human service providers in the District of Columbia were required to look at the health practices of the population at risk and how services are delivered to this population. To build a responsive and comprehensive delivery system necessitated the integration of the elements of public and private programs and services, resources, clients, and information in the community. Fortunately, community organization theory has been liberalized and social action strategies have been brought up to date by the inclusion of the concepts of political power and governmental influence.

Because no one person or discipline has all the skills and knowledge to manage a complex health problem such as infant mortality, an interdisciplinary team approach was instituted. The team, headed by a pediatrician (with training in neonatology) consisted of a social worker, nurse-midwife, health educator, nutritionist, and public health nurse. It focused on the community as the client, not only reaching out to meet its health needs, but being sensitive to other societal factors, including the need for housing, food, education, and family support systems. In addition, knowledge about the culture of a minority community was considered essential to understanding the community's functioning and dysfunctioning.

In the later stages of the IPO program, professionals with specialized skills in community organization and public awareness were recruited because of staff attrition and the limitations inherent in governmental programs, such as the lack of time, the inability to focus and concentrate on tasks, disincentives to be creative, and the lack of organized efforts to reach out to and follow up with clients. Contracts were undertaken with other agencies and consultants to provide services under the direction of a social work contract administrator. These consultants, who had special skills in utilizing the media and community education, were willing to work with community groups and residents late in the evenings and on holidays and weekends.

Through a systematic and continuous self-help process of community organization and development, outreach activities were developed to provide for the participation of community residents in addressing their community's needs on two levels: (1) via the existing providers of relevant health services and (2) via community residents and leaders. In turn, outreach strategies were implemented to improve and expand services for populations at risk of adverse pregnancy outcomes and to develop coalitions within the public and private sectors as a means of advancing the care of mothers and infants.

This basic process was instituted through suggested steps to foster community participation (see Fig. 1). Designated community groups and agencies were approached to provide their support for and participation in activities that would reduce infant mortality. In other words, the function of the facilitator–community organizer was to implement a set agenda for social action to prevent infant mortality. A problem-solving approach was instituted through negotiating shared goals and objectives in the public and private health care systems.

The process of finding solutions to infant mortality involved more than the social work goals of the steps in the process. As Murdach stated:

> A political approach to problem solving implies that clearly defining one's objectives, although important, may in the final analysis be less essential than the ability to mobilize the support necessary to their fulfillment. . . . A political perspective encourages. . .the negotiation of mutually beneficial settlements as a foundation on which further intervention can be based.[9]

Once the process of community involvement was activated, three basic techniques were tried to synthesize public and private responses: (1) coalition building and networking, (2) community education, and (3) target training.

Networks and Coalitions

The need for interaction among providers of services seemed especially pronounced because of the many needs of minority persons. The black community, in particular, has long relied on linking up and building support systems to meet its needs. Social relationships can be used as strengths—to gain assistance and advice. The environment, both internal and external, has provided for a natural multitude of formal and informal associations (or networks) that constitute a sense of community. Billingsley, Ladner, and Hill all studied strong kinship bonds and the adaptability of family roles of black people.[10] The IPO approach was successful because it incorporated the following formal and informal associations:

■ The family—in all its flexible definitions—is the primary helper of pregnant women. Then come natural peer groups, such as street-corner gangs, clubs, cliques, societies, school classes, and work-study groups.

■ The black church has served as a religious and social meeting place for the black community. Because its messages, delivered through its leadership, are usually accepted and respected, health activities in the church can be coordinated through this network.

■ Other associations in society, such as agencies, institutions, and the marketplace, expand the dimensions of community in people's lives by redefining nurturing as the utilization of health resources in the community for the benefit of children and their families. Connecting the value of health care with the value of nurturing in the black family has been a challenge to social work practitioners. Many institutions in the community, such as day care centers, make such connections daily with parents and children.

Coalition building can be interpreted as a task that is parallel to case coordination or case conferences which are held to serve multiproblem clients. A coalition of organizations just broadens this definition to include organizations in which representatives from agencies that serve a particular category of clients formally band together and agree to manage joint programs to deal with the clients' interdependent needs. Bender indicated that the boundaries of a community should be stretched to include shared experiences, mutual concerns, emotional bonds, and a common understanding and sense of obligations.[11]

In difficult economic times, coalitions and networks serve as advocates for increased and shared funding resources. Aiken et al. view coalitions of private and public organizations as powerful interest groups against which legislators have difficulty arguing because the coalitions can enlist a wide variety of support groups of clients.[12] Accordingly, in the IPO, coalitions of consumers and providers of services and advocates of health care were built around the issue of preventing infant mortality.

Community Education

IPO social workers engaged in community education on various levels using a variety of educational techniques. The challenge was

Figure 1.
Flexible Strategies for Community Participation

I. Initiate and direct a fact-finding project to provide baseline data on and resources for needs and problems of community groups.

    a. Focus on entry points by familiarizing oneself with the identified group of resources.

    b. Learn as much as possible about the functioning and rules of the formal and informal organizations.

    c. Learn about the agency's staff, particular problems, leadership style, and mode of operation.

    d. Learn about the legislative base, if pertinent.

II. Assess and analyze the findings to determine the next steps.

    a. Locate a sympathizer, cohort, and method of influence (policy, mandate, person).

    b. Evaluate traditional cultural values and how to determine how they fit in.

    c. Use findings (statistics, demographics) to select target groups.

    d. Determine groups' readiness to participate and gauge timing.

III. Initiate a communication system to foster joint planning.

    a. Recognize the parameters of the agency (where it fits in).

    b. Define roles and share definitions of the roles.

    c. Select appropriate vehicles of communication: weekly or monthly meetings, telephoning, memos, newsletters, and so forth.

    d. Document the system of communication and reinforce it.

IV. Structure the decision-making process. Determine and focus on the agenda through negotiating, redefining goals, and sharing information.

    a. Tending toward action.

        1. Nonideological.

        2. Limited distribution of costs, limited benefits, and limited scope.

        3. Flexible over time.

        4. Single focus for action.

        5. Consequences easily predictable.

        6. Features of issues easily communicable.

    b. Tending toward inaction.

        1. Highly ideological.

        2. Wide distribution of costs and benefits and wide scope.

        3. Irreversible, inflexible.

        4. Dispersed focus for action.

        5. Consequences uncertain.

        6. Issues abstract and complex.

Figure 1.
(Continued)

V. Interpret and translate the goals, objectives, and services of the agency in community terms. Consider the advantages and disadvantages to the agency.

VI. Provide leadership to focus on problems, resources, and decisions.
   a. Link the identification of problems to the development of goals that are selected.
   b. Develop the objectives of the program in relation to the organizational structure.
   c. Locate resources to take the proposed action.

VII. Bring together representatives of the community.
   a. Concentrate on those who have influence, who are committed, and who are in the position to commit others (getting the right representatives).

VIII. Begin joint planning. Collaborate in development of plans or utilize mechanisms for citizen participation.
   a. Education therapy strategy.
   b. Behavioral change strategy.
   c. Staff supplement strategy.
   d. Cooptation.
   e. Community power strategy.

IX. Choose the group method of coordination.
   a. Facilitate interdependence.
   b. Induce intervention by pooling power.
   c. Look at alternatives.

X. Assign tasks.

XI. Set up techniques to keep the program in operation.
   a. Develop a sense of unity.
   b. Set up a routine.
   c. Document.

XII. Pass on leadership.
   a. Identify natural group leaders.
   b. Allow their potential to grow.
   c. Retain their commitment through the liaison role.

---

to reach those persons who had dropped out of school, work, or the health care system. The following health messages were developed to be broadcast on radio or television: the need for pregnant women to seek early prenatal care, the importance of not smoking or abusing drugs or alcohol, and the need for good nutrition. A public awareness campaign, utilizing audio and visual messages, was tailored for effective communication to high-risk groups. Pamphlets and flyers also were distributed throughout the city.

The health care staff concentrated the distribution of information in public health clinics, libraries, physicians' offices, churches, public schools, day care centers, beauty salons, and grocery and department stores, where a variety of people could be reached. The staff also participated as speakers at health fairs, recreational and social events, and civic and community meetings, as well as on numerous radio and television programs.

Target Training

Target training, although an educational activity, differed from public awareness. The focus of the teaching was on the development of outreach skills, coupled with the provision of information on resources. Topics included a wide range of issues related to maternal and child health as well as subjects that would interest senior citizens, ministers, health workers, clerks in public health clinics, young men, and preschool and school-age children. Special programs on health-maintenance habits, continuing in school, the acquisition of skills, the planning of one's life, and the expansion of creative talents were aimed at increasing the self-esteem of minority children.[13] All participants were taught to negotiate the public health care system. After the completion of training, people in the community and agency staff members were encouraged to become missionaries of information about preventing infant mortality within their respective environments.

CONCLUSION

Reducing infant mortality in an urban black community is no easy or quick task. Because the problem and causes of infant mortality reflect the quality of life of black people, strategies have to be enacted that work through the underlying networks and institutions of a community, as well as its politics. Social workers have an opportunity to intervene in schools, day care centers, housing projects, churches, and social and civic groups through community organization, community education, and community outreach. Together, these strategies can foster a recognition of interdependence, an exchange of information, and, most important, a commitment to promote the well-being of all constituents. Social action can occur by negotiating an agenda whose focus is on preventing the death of infants.

Building on the natural linkages and the value of nurturing in the black community, the social work facilitator can reach some of those who have dropped out of the health care system. He or she also can help stimulate partnership and the sharing of public and private resources. Finally, promoting the awareness of health and health care services through community participation may stimulate a reinterpretation of the self-help process in social work practice.

Notes and References

1. Select Panel for the Promotion of Child, *Better Health for Our Children: A National Strategy.* Vol. 1: *Major Findings and Recommendations,* Vol. IV: *A Statistical Profile* (Washington, D.C.: U.S. Government Printing Office, 1981).

2. Warren W. Morse, *Infant Mortality and Related Live Birth Characteristics: District of Columbia* (Washington, D.C.: Office of Policy and Planning, Department of Human Services, District of Columbia, October 1982).

3. Joan Maxwell, *The Prevention of Prematurity: A Strategy to Reduce Infant Mortality in the District of Columbia* (Washington, D.C.: Greater Washington Research Center, November 1982), pp. 3–4.

4. Ibid., pp. 7–8.

5. Morse, *Infant Mortality and Related Live Birth Characteristics.*

6. Margaret S. Boone, "A Socio-Medical Study of Infant Mortality among Disadvantaged Blacks," *Human Organization,* 41 (1982), p. 227.

7. Barbara J. Hatcher et al., "Improved Pregnancy Outcome Project." Paper presented at the 108th Annual Meeting of the American Public Health Association, Detroit, Michigan, October 22, 1980.

8. Lydia Rapoport, "The Concept of Prevention in Social Work," *Social Work,* 6 (January 1961), pp. 3–12.

9. Allison D. Murdach, "A Political Perspective in Problem Solving," *Social Work,* 27 (September 1982), pp. 419–420.

10. Andrew Billingsley, *Black Families and the Struggle for Survival* (New York: Friendship Publishing, 1974); Joyce A. Ladner, *Tomorrow's Tomorrow: The Black Woman* (New York: Doubleday & Co., 1971); and Robert Hill, *Strengths of Black Families* (New York: Emerson Hall Publishers, 1972).

11. Thomas Bender, *Community and Social Change in America* (New Brunswick, N.J.: Rutgers University Press, 1978).

12. Michael Aiken et al., *Coordinating Human Services: New Strategies for Building Service Delivery Systems* (San Francisco: Jossey-Bass, 1975).

13. Naomi H. Chamberlain, "Partners in Teaching Community Health," *Public Health Reports,* 91 (May–June 1976), pp. 268–270.